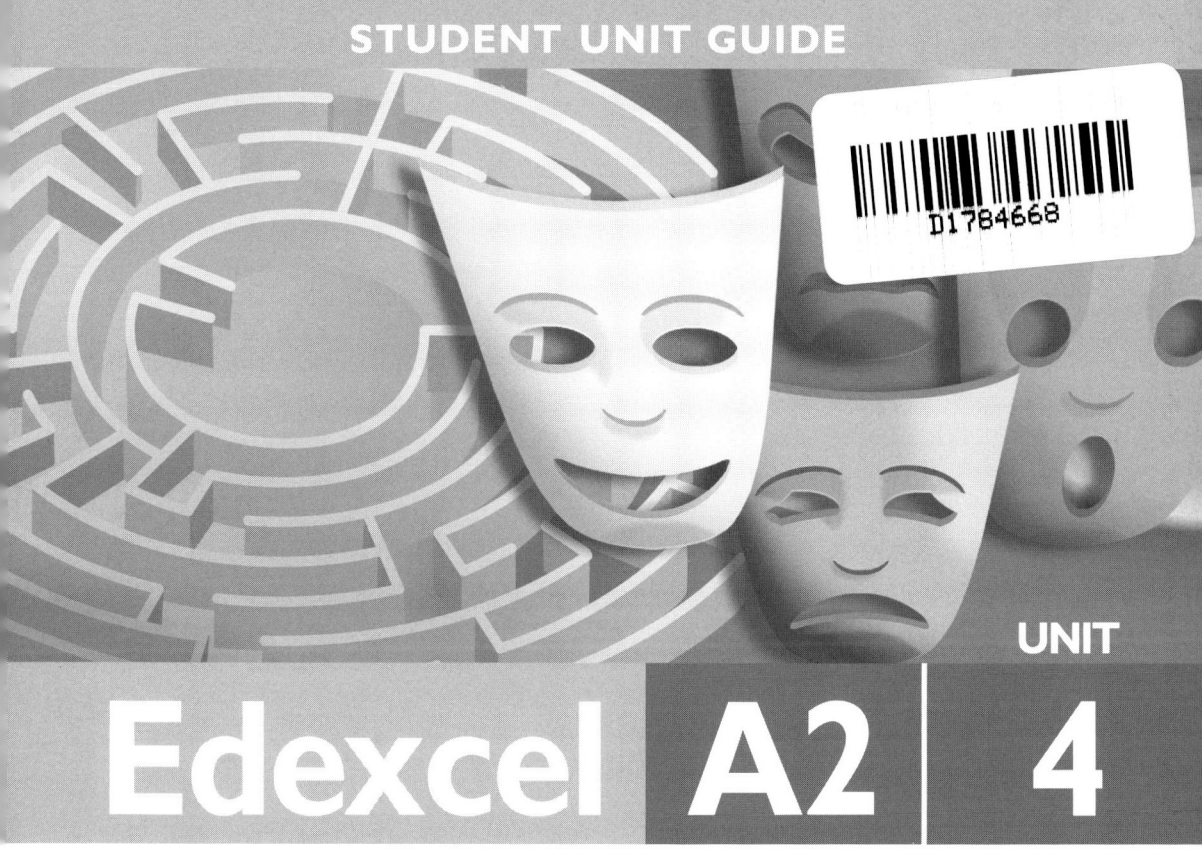

Edexcel A2 | UNIT 4

Psychology
How Psychology Works

Christine Brain

Philip Allan Updates, an imprint of Hodder Education, an Hachette UK company, Market Place, Deddington, Oxfordshire OX15 0SE

Orders

Bookpoint Ltd, 130 Milton Park, Abingdon, Oxfordshire OX14 4SB

tel: 01235 827720

fax: 01235 400454

e-mail: uk.orders@bookpoint.co.uk

Lines are open 9.00 a.m.–5.00 p.m., Monday to Saturday, with a 24-hour message answering service. You can also order through the Philip Allan Updates website: www.philipallan.co.uk

© Philip Allan Updates 2010

ISBN 978-0-340-94923-8

First printed 2010

Impression number 5 4 3 2

Year 2014 2013 2012 2011 2010

This guide has been written specifically to support students preparing for the Edexcel A2 Psychology Unit 4 examination. The content has been neither approved nor endorsed by Edexcel and remains the sole responsibility of the author.

Typeset by DC Graphic Design Ltd, Swanley Village, Kent

Printed by MPG Books, Bodmin

Hachette UK's policy is to use papers that are natural, renewable and recyclable products and made from wood grown in sustainable forests. The logging and manufacturing processes are expected to conform to the environmental regulations of the country of origin.

Contents

Introduction

■ ■ ■

Content Guidance

■ ■ ■

Questions and Answers

Introduction

About this guide

This is a guide to Unit 4 of the Edexcel A2 specification, How Psychology Works. The unit is made up of two parts: Clinical Psychology and Issues and Debates.

This introductory section covers ideas of how to use the guide and points about the exam. A content section follows, covering the material you need to know — though you will need to add more depth, as this guide is a summary. Finally, there is a question and answer section, with examiner advice, to help you with your revision.

If you have covered the material in class, attended reasonably well and done some work of your own, you should do well in this unit. Even if you feel you don't know much about the Unit 4 material, keep calm; read through this guide carefully, using the questions and answers as you go to reinforce your learning, and you can still do well.

You can make positive use of your exam experiences from the AS units and Unit 3. You will already know how to answer the questions; for example what 'describe' means and what 'evaluate' asks for. The Unit 4 exam paper follows a very similar structure to the one for Unit 3 (which itself is very similar to those for the two AS units). For example, essay questions are marked using levels that look at the quality of your answer, and how well you have communicated and used relevant terms, rather than using point-by-point marking.

Note that this guide is not a textbook — there is no substitute for reading the required material and taking notes. It does not tell you the actual questions on your paper, or give you the answers!

Aims of the guide

The aim of this guide is to provide you with a clear understanding of the requirements of Unit 4 of the A2 specification and to advise you on how best to meet these requirements.

This guide will look at:
- the psychology you need to know about
- what you need to be able to do and what skills you need
- how you could go about learning the necessary material
- what is being examined
- what you should expect in the examination for this unit
- how you could tackle the different styles of exam question
- the format of the exam, including what questions might look like

- how questions are marked, including examples of answers, with examiner's comments

How to use this guide

A good way to use this guide is to read it through in the order in which it is presented. Alternatively, you can consider each topic in the Content Guidance section, and then turn to the relevant question in the Question and Answer section. Whichever way you use the guide, try some of the questions yourself to test your learning. You should know enough about the marking by this time to try to grade your own answers. If you are working with someone else, mark each other's answers. The more you work on what is needed, the better. Have other textbooks available too — you will need access to all the relevant information.

Study skills and revision strategies

Before reading on, answer the following questions:
- How long is left before the exam?
- Do you have a revision plan?
- Are you sure you want to pass, and hopefully do well? Renewing your motivation can help.
- Are you stressed and in a panic?
- Can you stick to your plan, and trust it?

If you need to, draw up a revision plan now, remind yourself that you do want to succeed, and practise some relaxation techniques.

Revision plan
- Start at least 4 weeks before the exam date (sooner if possible).
- Using times that suit you (6 a.m. might be a great time to study!), draw up a blank timetable for each of the weeks.
- On the timetable, fill in all your urgent commitments (cancel as many plans as you can).
- Divide up what is left, allocating slots to all your subjects as appropriate. Don't forget to build in meal times, breaks and time for sleep.
- Stick to the plan if at all possible, but if you have to, amend it as you go.
- When studying, have frequent, short rests and no distractions.

Time management

Answer the following questions to see how good you are at time management.

(1) Are you usually punctual?
    yes   no

(2) Do you tend to work fast and then correct mistakes?

yes   no

(3) Do you often put things off?

yes   no

(4) Do you feel stressed because you never have enough time?

yes   no

(5) Do you work slowly and carefully, and try to get things right first time?

yes   no

(6) Do you daydream?

yes   no

(7) Are you forgetful?

yes   no

(8) Do you find it hard to get started?

yes   no

(9) Do you keep your desk tidy?

yes   no

Score 0 for 'yes' and 1 for 'no' to questions 1, 5 and 9. Score 1 for 'yes' and 0 for 'no' to questions 2, 3, 4, 6, 7 and 8. A score of 3 or below means your time management is quite good; a score of 4 and above means you need to work on it.

Relaxation techniques

The following boxes suggest some ways to relax. Use these as appropriate.

Technique 1 — takes about 10 minutes

This technique is useful at the start or end of a longish revision period.
- Lie on the floor and make yourself comfortable.
- Working from toes to head, tense each of your muscles in turn and then relax.
- Having relaxed your body, now relax your thoughts.
- Take yourself in your mind to a place where you feel at peace — this could be a favourite holiday place, or a favourite place on a walk. Closing your eyes will help.
- Have a good look around (mentally), sit down there and listen to the sounds of the place.
- Stay there and try not to come back yet.
- When you are ready, come back. Slowly start to hear the sounds around you, and lie with your body relaxed for a little while longer.

Technique 2 — takes about 5 minutes

This technique is useful as you revise. Work for between 30 minutes and an hour, and then stop to relax as follows:

- Sit comfortably and try to ignore anything going on around you.
- Imagine you are in a barn, sitting on the rafters under the roof, swinging your legs and sitting comfortably. Closing your eyes will help.
- Now, imagine that the barn has open doors at both ends, and there is a river rushing through from one end of the barn to the other. You are sitting swinging your legs, watching the river rush through below you.
- Hear the water rushing through, sit comfortably, and just watch.
- Think of the water as your thoughts rushing away.
- You are not involved, just watching.
- After about 3 minutes or when you are ready, slowly start to hear the sounds around you, and gradually bring your thoughts back into the real world. Look around you for a minute or two and check that you feel better, before getting back to work.

Technique 3 — takes about 1 minute

This technique is useful when you are actually in the examination, and can be used if you are too anxious to continue.

- Imagine you are in an exam now.
- Imagine that you are getting anxious.
- Pick up a pen as if to write.
- Hold the pen up in front of you and stare at it.
- Let all your other thoughts go and think about the pen.
- Try to think of nothing else even for a few seconds.
- Get back to work!

Use your knowledge of psychology to relax

If you covered cognitive behavioural therapy in your course then use some of those techniques for yourself. For example, the idea is that thinking leads to emotions that lead to behaviour, which tends to have consequences that lead to a vicious cycle. So if you think 'I can't cope', this will cause feelings like anxiety, fear and sadness. These feelings will lead to behaviour such as not revising, trying to do too much, or withdrawing from family and friends. The consequences are likely to be that you do even less, so think even more that you cannot cope, and that you get no support from others to help you to think differently. This is a vicious cycle that is not helpful. Better thoughts would be 'I can cope with some revision' or 'I can at least pass' or 'Of course I can cope, I have done it before'.

Remember that stress is thinking that you don't have the resources to cope — it involves thinking and CBT is useful in changing thinking. Stop being negative and telling yourself you don't have the resources to pass — replace with healthier thoughts such as 'Yes I do have the resources' or 'I have got this far so I can't be that bad in exams'.

Examination structure and skills

Unit 4 is in two parts. The first part is clinical psychology, which is an application — you have already covered two applications for Unit 3. The second part is called 'Issues and Debates' and draws together your learning over the course. For example, you are asked about the main research methods, the key issues you have covered through the course and other issues such as nature–nurture.

There will be one whole question for each of the two parts (clinical psychology and issues/debates), which will be divided into separate parts. Clinical psychology, as with the Unit 3 applications, has five parts — definitions, methodology, content, studies in detail, and key issue/practical. There will not be a question for each part of the application — questions will range across these five areas.

Exam structure and assessment objectives (AOs)

Each of the two A2 exam papers (for Units 3 and 4) has some short answer questions, some extended writing questions, and essay questions. Units 1, 2 and 3 have had a 12-mark essay at the end but Unit 4 includes what is expected to be a 12-mark essay at the end of the clinical psychology section, and a longer essay at the end of the issues and debates section.

The assessment objectives (AOs) of the A2 exam papers are the same as for the AS papers. Briefly, they are as follows (they are explained more fully below):
- AO1 — testing knowledge with understanding and good communication skills
- AO2 — testing evaluation, assessment and applications
- AO3 — testing understanding and evaluation of methodology, including other people's studies

Don't think that someone sets each paper with past papers in front of them, avoiding what has been asked before. Imagine someone trying to set an interesting paper, covering a range of topics from the five areas for the application and the material in issues/debates, and balancing AO1, AO2 and AO3 marks according to the required percentages of each. It is not possible to guess what will be on the paper — don't try. Prepare answers for all possible questions. The only guarantee is that there will be the two types of question (short answer and extended writing) and an essay question at the end of each whole question.

Expect the mark allocation for the essay at the end of the clinical psychology whole question to be 12 marks and expect the essay question at the end of the issues/debates section to have 18 marks available. For the issues/debates section only, you should expect a choice of two questions (each with the 18 marks).

Different people set the papers, and there are not as many strict rules about setting the papers as you might think. Tips in this guide include words such as 'usually'. Each paper will be different, and you have to be prepared to answer whatever questions appear. For example, there are many ways that short answer questions can be written, such as:

- 'Explain what is meant by...'
- 'Describe the procedure of...'
- 'Outline the theory...'
- 'Outline two weaknesses of...'
- 'Compare two explanations...'

Read the question carefully and do what is asked, and you will do well.

Assessment objectives in more detail

The assessment objectives are listed in the specification. A brief explanation is given below, but check the full list of what you will be assessed on.

Assessment objective 1: knowledge and understanding (AO1)

- You need to recognise, recall and show understanding of psychological knowledge, including theories, studies, methods and concepts, as well as psychological principles, perspectives and applications.
- You must communicate clearly and effectively, and present and select material well. For example, if you are asked to explain what is meant by validity (clinical psychology) for 2 marks, and you just say that it is about real-life data, you have not explained enough. You need to make your points clearly — for example:

  'Validity with regard to a clinical diagnosis is about the diagnosis being real in the sense of being what it claims to be. For example, if someone is diagnosed with schizophrenia because of having hallucinations, but they are having hallucinations because of medication they are on, then the diagnosis of schizophrenia is not valid.'

- You may lose marks by using bullet points, so avoid them. The problem with bullet points is that they encourage shorthand, meaning that your answer will not be clearly and effectively communicated.

Assessment objective 2: evaluation and comment (AO2)

You must be able to:

- analyse and evaluate psychological theories and concepts, referring to relevant evidence
- apply psychological knowledge and understanding to unfamiliar situations
- assess the validity, reliability and credibility of psychological knowledge

Assessment objective 3 (AO3)

You must:

- be able to describe ethical, safe and skilful practical techniques and processes, including selecting appropriate qualitative and quantitative methods
- know how to make, record and communicate reliable and valid measurements, using primary and secondary sources
- be able to analyse, explain, interpret and evaluate methodology, results and impact of both your own practicals and the studies of others

The Unit 4 exam

Unit 4 is assessed in a 2-hour exam. Answers are written in a booklet similar to those used at GCSE. There are 90 marks available. This means you need to score around 1 mark per minute, with 30 minutes to spare for reading and thinking. In general, you can expect to gain 1 mark for each point that answers the question, or for elaboration of a point. Answers must be communicated 'clearly and effectively' (see AO1 above). Avoid one-word answers unless they are asked for. The final essay question for clinical psychology is expected to be worth 12 marks; the final essay question for issues/debates is expected to be worth 18 marks, with a choice of two titles.

Overall, marks are awarded as follows:
- About 26% of the marks (around 24 marks when considering both parts of Unit 4) are awarded for knowledge and understanding (AO1).
- About 50% (around 45 marks when considering both parts of Unit 4) are for evaluation and comment and application to unfamiliar situations (AO2).
- About 24% (around 21 marks when considering both parts of Unit 4) are for knowledge and assessment of practical work, both your own and other people's.

In practice you can simply focus on revising equal amounts of AO1, AO2 and AO3 (knowledge, evaluation and practical work) and just answer each question as it arises.

Two types of marking

There are two types of marking. One type is point-based marking, where 1 mark is awarded per point made, and there are also marks for elaboration of a point. The other type of marking involves 'levels', which means there are bands of marks that are awarded according to the quality of the answer. An example is the following mark scheme for a question asking for the IV for a study for 2 marks:
- 0 marks — no appropriate material (e.g. giving the DV)
- 1 mark — not fully operationalised (e.g. giving one side of the IV)
- 2 marks — fully operationalised, giving both or all sides of the IV, and possibly an example

Questions about your own practicals are marked according to levels and quality — for example, if you are asked about planning your leaflet, a thorough answer will get full marks and a weak answer will get very few marks.

The essays are also marked using levels and according to quality. For example, if you are asked about two treatments for schizophrenia and you only discuss one treatment, you will be in the middle band somewhere. It is in the levels marking that your writing skills are assessed, including how well you select material for your answer, and the quality of your spelling, grammar and use of terminology.

AO1, AO2 and AO3: getting it right

You must be sure to answer the question that is set — you should then cover the AO1, AO2 and/or AO3 skills. The key words in the question (e.g. 'outline'), called **injunctions**, guide what you need to write. If you answer the question, you will automatically do what is required without worrying about the various assessment objectives.

Table 1 shows some examples of how AO1 injunctions are used and Table 2 shows examples of AO2 injunctions. Table 3 shows some examples of AO3 questions, which can include various kinds of injunctions but must be about practicals and methodology in some way. Note that it is not so much the word itself (e.g. 'describe') as the whole question that makes it AO1, AO2 or AO3. The figures in brackets suggest the mark allocation you might expect for such a question.

Table 1 Examples of AO1 questions/injunctions

Type of question	What is being asked for
Describe a theory... (5)	Say what something is (a theory in this case). Imagine describing the theory to someone who knows little about the subject.
Identify a treatment... (1)	Give enough information so that the examiner can understand what is being referred to. For example, if asked to identify a treatment from the social approach you might say 'care in the community'.
Identify a study... (1)	Name either the study or the psychologist(s). For example, if the question asks for a study, the answer might be 'Rosenhan (1973)' or 'on being sane in insane places'.
Outline a definition of the ... application (3)	Follow the instructions for 'describe', but remember that this injunction requires less detail, and hence carries fewer marks.

Table 2 Examples of AO2 questions/injunctions

Type of question	What is being asked for
Outline a strength of... (2)	You are asked to outline something, so the injunction seems to be AO1 (i.e. knowledge and understanding). However, as what is outlined is a *strength* (in this case), and thus you are being asked to evaluate something, this question would carry AO2 marks.
With regard to the stimulus material above, explain... (6)	You are asked to refer to some stimulus material and apply your knowledge of psychology to explain the material in some way. Refer to the material at least once in your answer.
Compare two explanations for schizophrenia... (6)	You are asked to choose two explanations for schizophrenia and then write about how they are similar and/or how they are different. 'And/or' means you can do both or one or the other.
Assess how far a treatment used in clinical psychology is successful... (4)	You are asked to consider one treatment and suggest how successful it is. You should also identify any ways in which it is unsuccessful so you can come to an overall conclusion about its success. You are asked to evaluate treatments and not precisely about their effectiveness. This question is broad and you can choose the treatment, so it is reasonable to expect that you know something about one treatment's effectiveness.

Table 3 Examples of AO3 questions/injunctions

Type of question	What is being asked for
Outline the aim(s) of your leaflet... (2)	You are asked to say what the purpose of your practical was; that is, to say briefly what you were trying to explain. 'Outline' sounds like an AO1 injunction, but as this is about your practical, it is an AO3 question.
Evaluate one study you have covered in clinical psychology — either Rosenhan (1973) or one of the two other studies you have done (one for schizophrenia and one for your other chosen disorder). (6)	You have to have covered Rosenhan (1973) and two others. Choose one you know well and give comments, criticisms, good points and so on. Consider strengths and weaknesses of the research method, perhaps, or criticisms of the ethics involved. Look at alternative findings or consider whether justified conclusions are drawn. Although 'evaluate' sounds like an AO2 injunction, the question is about someone else's study, which is psychology in practice, so it is an AO3 question.

Conclusions: use of injunctions and the AO1/AO2/AO3 split

Don't just think of a word in the question as being the whole question. For example, you might think 'describe' is an AO1 command because it seems to ask for knowledge. However, 'describe a strength...' is an AO2 injunction because it asks for evaluation; and 'describe the procedure of your practical (leaflet production)' is an AO3 question because it asks about psychology in practice. 'Discuss' could signal AO2 marks if you are asked to 'discuss the usefulness of...': because you are considering how useful something is, you are doing more than showing knowledge about it. The best approach is to *answer the question*. If you pay careful attention to the question so that you understand what it asks you to do, all should be well.

The specification gives a list of what injunction words mean in your course, so you could look at that to check your understanding. However, the question should indicate clearly what you have to do. Remember that the specification, sample papers and sample mark scheme are on the Edexcel website. Table 4 shows how marks are split between the assessment objectives for each unit of the A-level.

Table 4 Approximate mark allocation AO1/AO2/AO3 for the whole A-level

	AO1	AO2	AO3	Total
AS Unit 1	8%	6%	6%	20%
AS Unit 2	12%	9%	9%	30%
A2 Unit 3	6%	8%	6%	20%
A2 Unit 4	9%	14%	7%	30%
Total	**35%**	**37%**	**28%**	**100%**

You can see that, for the two AS units, you were assessed more on your knowledge and understanding (40%) than on your ability to comment and evaluate (30%). For Unit 3, you were assessed more on your ability to comment and evaluate (40%) than on your knowledge and understanding (30%). For Unit 4, your knowledge and understanding and your evaluation and comment skills are assessed differently as well, with AO1 taking up 25–30% of the unit and AO2 taking up 45–50% of the unit. So the two A2 units have noticeably more AO2 than AO1, with AO3 staying roughly the same.

Essentially, then, you have to learn material so you know and understand it, and then plan some criticisms, comments and evaluation points. As a rule of thumb, be sure to learn or plan as many evaluation and comment points as you learn information points.

Differences between AS and A2

Although a lot of what is true for AS still applies to A2 — for example, the AO1, AO2 and AO3 assessment objectives — the A2 exams require higher-level skills. At A2, more marks are given for AO2 (evaluation and comment) than for AO1 (knowledge and understanding). This is different from what is required at AS. It means you need to comment, evaluate, assess, consider strengths, and so on, more than you need to give information. When you are making notes and preparing answers to exam questions, remember to concentrate on criticisms. Whenever you read an evaluation point, note it down and learn it.

Greater depth is also required in your answers at A2. For example, you could be asked about two contributions from the cognitive approach. The specification does not say that you need studies and evidence, but they could be useful. Remember to refer to the assessment objectives outlined in this introduction. The specification might not ask you specifically to learn studies regarding care in the community (if you choose it as a treatment from the social approach), but you will need to refer to relevant evidence to support your answers (AO2). Psychology is built on evidence from studies, so when revising it is useful to have a list of names of studies and a brief outline of what each is about. Note also that Unit 4 (the clinical application) is about applications of psychology, so be ready to apply your knowledge.

Content
Guidance

This section provides an overview of what you need to learn for Unit 4, the Clinical Psychology application and a section called Issues and Debates. It includes some AO1 (knowledge and understanding) material for each topic, as well as AO2 evaluation points. There are also AO3 points, which are about methodology and how science and psychology work.

The clinical psychology section is divided into the following areas:
- Summary of what you need to know
- Definition of the application
- Methodology and how science works
- Content
- Studies in detail
- Evidence in practice: key issue and practical

The section on issues and debates is organised as follows:
- Introduction to issues and debates
- Definitions
- Contributions
- Ethics
- Methods
- Key issues
- Debates
- New situations

Clinical psychology

Summary of what you need to know

In this study guide, choices are made for you, to limit the material. However, if you have studied a different choice it is probably better to revise that, rather than learn something new at this stage.

Definition of the application

- You need to know what clinical psychology is about — that it involves explaining and treating mental illness.
- You should be able to define some key terms: statistical definition of abnormality, social norm definition of abnormality, schizophrenia, reliability, validity, primary data and secondary data.

Methodology and how science works

- You need to know about primary and secondary data and be able to evaluate their use, as well as explain how issues of validity and reliability arise in clinical psychology.
- You should be able to describe and evaluate two research methods used to study schizophrenia, with a study for each method.

Content

- You need to know two definitions of abnormality (statistical deviation and social norm), and be able to evaluate them in terms of how suitable they are as definitions of abnormality.
- Using studies, you should be able to describe and evaluate issues of validity, reliability and culture with regard to diagnosing mental disorders. This must involve the use of the DSM.
- You need to study schizophrenia and one other disorder (selected from unipolar depression, bipolar depression, phobias, obsessive compulsive disorder, anorexia nervosa and bulimia nervosa). You should be able to describe the features and symptoms of both disorders.
- For schizophrenia, you need to know a biological explanation and another explanation from one of the other four AS approaches. For the other disorder, you also need to know two explanations, taken from two of the AS approaches.
- For both schizophrenia and your other chosen disorder, you need to be able to describe and evaluate two treatments.

- You also have to know one treatment from each of the AS approaches and there are two options in each approach to choose from. Some of these treatments you may have covered when looking at schizophrenia and your other disorder, so just add the others as necessary.

Studies in detail

- The required study is Rosenhan (1973), 'On being sane in insane places'.
- You also need to be able to describe and evaluate one study about schizophrenia and one study about your other chosen disorder.

Evidence in practice: short practical — drawing up a leaflet

You need to be able to describe a key issue in clinical psychology covering an area from the specification and also to prepare a leaflet about the key issue, using secondary sources. There has to be a commentary on the leaflet explaining your decisions, who the audience was and what the intended outcomes were.

Definition of the application

Clinical psychology is about diagnosing, explaining and treating mental disorders such as schizophrenia and bipolar depression. To explain more about what clinical psychologists might do, use what follows in the content section about schizophrenia and bipolar depression, as well as what you have learned about problems with defining abnormality, such as difficulties with the reliability and validity of the DSM. For example, explanations for mental disorders can be biological, looking at genes or brain functioning, or they can be social, looking at how interactions with others can affect mental functioning.

Key terms that you need to be able to define are explained later: statistical definition of abnormality (pp. 27–29), social norm definition of abnormality (pp. 29–30), schizophrenia (pp. 38–40), reliability (p. 21), validity (p. 21), primary data and secondary data (p. 19).

Methodology and how science works

This section first explains about primary and secondary data and their uses. This is followed by a brief discussion of the issues of validity and reliability in clinical psychology (more detail on this is given in the content section later). The last part of the section describes two methods used to study schizophrenia, which is one of the mental disorders explained later.

Primary and secondary data

In this section both types of data are described and then evaluated.

Primary data

- **Primary data** (a key term) are gathered first-hand from source.
- They are gathered by the researcher.
- They are for the purpose that they are intended.
- Milgram (1963) gathered primary data when noting the voltage at which a participant stopped 'giving a shock' to someone.
- Bandura et al. (1961) gathered primary data when measuring aggressive behaviour of children who had watched various examples of aggressive behaviour (or not).
- Observations, case studies, questionnaires, interviews and experiments are all ways of gathering primary data.

Secondary data

- **Secondary data** (a key term) are data that someone has already gathered, which means they are 'second-hand'.
- They are for the purpose of the researcher(s) who gathered them.
- They are then used by someone else for the purpose of their own research, which is likely to be different from the original purpose.
- They can come from government sources, such as statistics of deprivation in an area or information about daycare.
- A meta-analysis uses secondary data, because a meta-analysis is an analysis of many different studies focused on the same hypothesis or area, so it draws on the findings of those different studies to draw an overall conclusion. This means that data are not usually gathered directly as well.
- Secondary data will originally have been gathered by means of observations, case studies, questionnaires, interviews and experiments, and will originally have been primary data; however, they become secondary when used in another study.

Using both types of data

Gottesman and Shields (1966) (pp. 22–24) used both types of data in their study to see if schizophrenia is inherited. First, they found out about the mental health of pairs of identical and non-identical twins by accessing hospital records for twins where at least one of the pair had been diagnosed with a mental disorder. This was using secondary data. Then they interviewed the twins, as adults, to assess their mental health and to find out the course of their mental disorder. When interviewing they were gathering primary data. They gathered quite a lot of information about the twins and then drew conclusions about how often, when one twin had schizophrenia or some related disorder, the other had been diagnosed with it as well.

Tip

This study is useful when you study schizophrenia and also as an example of a research method called a 'twin study', which is also part of this application.

Evaluation of the use of primary and secondary data in research

The following points are set out as comparison points to help you to answer questions that ask you to compare.

Strengths of primary over secondary data

- Primary data are better because they are gathered for the intended purpose and so are likely to be more focused on that purpose, whereas secondary data are taken from another source and have often been gathered for a different reason. For example, Gottesman and Shields (1966) had to discount some of the pairs of twins because they could not be sure whether they were monozygotic or dizygotic (MZ or DZ) twins, which affected their study. If they had gathered primary data, they would have been more likely to get all the information they needed.
- Primary data tend to be more valid in that they are gathered first-hand and any operationalising is done carefully with the purpose in mind so the data are more likely to represent real life. Secondary data, if they are statistics from surveys, which they often are, might not be valid if used as if they are about individuals. However, if secondary data were originally primary data from another study, then they might well have been gathered validly. When secondary data are gathered for one purpose and used for another this can affect their validity.
- Primary data are more likely to have credibility as they are gathered for the specific purpose and analysed with that purpose in mind. Secondary data are likely to have been gathered with one purpose in mind and when used in a 'secondary' fashion (which is when they become secondary data) they may not be seen to have credibility.
- Primary data are analysed directly by the researcher(s), whereas secondary data may already have been analysed, which can bring in an element of subjectivity. However, secondary data can be 'raw' data and not previously analysed.
- Primary data are gathered at the time of the study, whereas secondary data are likely to have been gathered some time previously, which means that primary data are more likely to be valid in the sense of being up to date.

Strengths of secondary over primary data

- Secondary data are cheaper because they are already there. Primary data tend to be expensive because the study has to be run completely, including finding the participants, developing the research method and setting up any situation or survey.
- Secondary data can use more participants, such as in a meta-analysis, so the range of participants can be wider and generalisability can be improved. This is not always the case, but in studies such as Craft et al. (2003), where they used data from many studies that used the same questionnaire, they had a lot more data than if they had gathered the information first-hand. Studies gathering primary data are often limited in the number of people they involve.
- Secondary data tends to gather more data too, although again this is not always the case. For example, Gottesman and Shields (1966), by using the hospital records

over a number of years, were able to access a lot of detail about pairs of twins that otherwise would have been hard, if not impossible, to put together. When gathering primary data it is often the case that the numbers that can be involved are limited, either by cost or to make the study manageable, or both.

Tips

- When asked to compare you should always give both sides for each point — do not just say 'and the other one is not', but clearly show both sides of the comparison point.

- You need to be able to evaluate the use of primary and secondary data when doing research, so evaluation of Gottesman and Shields (1966) is useful. Gottesman and Shields (1966) is chosen here as an example of a study of schizophrenia, so learn it for that purpose as well and then use evaluation points of the study as appropriate when discussing the use of primary and secondary data.

Issues of reliability and validity in clinical psychology

This section gives a brief overview of the issues of reliability and validity and how they arise within clinical psychology. These issues are discussed in more detail with regard to diagnoses in the content section later.

Briefly, **validity** (a key term) is found when something is measuring what it claims to measure — when the measurement is about real life. For example, say a doctor diagnoses someone with unipolar depression (pp. 48–56) and they are treated for that mental disorder. The treatment is not likely to work if they are suffering from bipolar disorder (manic depression) and in that case, the first diagnosis would not have been valid, which led to inappropriate treatment.

Reliability (a key term) is found when something found once is found again — there is consistency in findings where the measurement is the same. For example, if different doctors separately diagnose the same patient, who presents with the same symptoms, as having unipolar depression, then the diagnosis seems reliable. However, if different doctors diagnose the same person as having different mental disorders (e.g. unipolar and bipolar depression), then the diagnoses are not reliable and, therefore, not useful.

Two research methods used to study schizophrenia

The two methods chosen here are twin studies and interviewing, though there are many research methods used to study schizophrenia, including animal experiments, case studies, and biological methods such as scanning. For each of the research methods you need to know a study to illustrate the relevant method.

Tip

If you studied a different research method from twin studies or interviewing, you might prefer to revise that method instead of learning another one.

Twin studies to study schizophrenia

Twin studies involve using identical (monozygotic or MZ) twins and non-identical (dizygotic or DZ) twins and then comparing them in some way.

Brothers and sisters in a family share 50% of their genes, as do non-identical (DZ) twins. DZ twins come from two eggs. MZ (identical) twins, however, come from one egg (monozygotic means 'one egg') and share 100% of their genes.

This difference in how many genes DZ and MZ twins share is the key to the research method. With MZ twins, as 100% of the genes are in common, any difference found between the twins is thought to come from environmental factors. Therefore twin studies are very helpful as evidence in the nature–nurture debate (pp. 86–87) because what MZ twins have in common is likely to come from nature and how they differ is likely to come from nurture.

In practice MZ twins are not completely alike (for example, they have different fingerprint patterns) and it is not expected that they would share any characteristic exactly. So what twin studies look for is where MZ twins share a characteristic a lot more than DZ twins share it.

In research on schizophrenia, studies look at how often, when one twin has schizophrenia, the other has it too. If schizophrenia has a genetic cause in any way then MZ twins should be more likely to both have schizophrenia when one has it than DZ twins. This is in fact what studies find, for example Gottesman and Shields (1966).

You may have covered Gottesman and Shields (1966) for the biological approach in the AS part of your course — if so, review that material.

Strengths and weaknesses of twin studies

Strengths	Weaknesses
• There is no other way to study genetic influences so clearly, because no other humans share 100% of their DNA	• MZ twins share their DNA but even in the womb they may experience different environments, which may lead them to develop differently
• Although the extent to which they share their DNA differs, both MZ and DZ twins share their environments, so there is a natural control over environmental effects	• MZ twins may be treated more alike than DZ twins because they are identical and share their gender too, so their environments may not be as controlled as might be thought

Gottesman and Shields (1966)

Aims

Gottesman and Shields (1966) wanted to find out how far schizophrenia is genetic. They wanted to try to replicate other studies that had found a genetic link.

Procedure

They gathered secondary data from a hospital in the USA and found twins where at least one had been diagnosed with schizophrenia. This was from 1948 over 16 years. From 392 patients they found 68 who were one of twins and had a diagnosis of schizophrenia or related psychosis. They included 62 patients in the study for various reasons (31 males and 31 females) and in fact this gave 57 pairs, because in 5 cases both twins were in the sample (as both had been diagnosed with schizophrenia).

The researchers tracked down both twins in each pair. Blood tests and visual tests were used to see if they were MZ or DZ twins and many methods were used to collect data, such as hospital notes and case histories (secondary data), and tape recordings of interview data (primary data). There was also personality testing and a test to look at thought disorders (primary data). As well as recording whether the participants had had a diagnosis of schizophrenia, the researchers looked at related psychoses, and also used their data to make judgements about the mental health of participants.

They looked at the concordance rate, which is how often, when one of a pair has a diagnosis of schizophrenia (or related disorder), the other one has it too. They divided the results according to whether a pair was DZ or MZ and then they could see if the concordance rate was higher for MZ twins, which was what they expected.

Results

- Of the MZ pairs of twins where one was diagnosed with schizophrenia, the other also had a schizophrenia diagnosis in 42% of cases (10 pairs). For the DZ twins the figure was 9% (3 pairs).
- The concordance rates were higher when diagnoses of disorders closely related to schizophrenia were included as well. For MZ twins the rate was 54% (13 pairs), and for the DZ twins it was 18% (6 pairs).
- When the most severe cases of schizophrenia were looked at, the concordance rate for MZ twins was between 75% and 91%, which is very high.

Conclusions

There was evidence from the study that MZ twins were more likely to both have a diagnosis of schizophrenia and related disorders than DZ twins, which is evidence of a genetic link. This is particularly true for severe cases of schizophrenia.

However, as it was not the case that in every pair both twins had schizophrenia, then this is not 100% genetic and environmental factors presumably play a part too. The researchers favoured the diathesis–stress explanation, which holds that a person may have a tendency towards developing schizophrenia (a genetic predisposition) but that environmental triggers also seem to play a part. Particular genes may predispose someone to schizophrenia and that predisposition perhaps lowers the threshold for coping with stress.

The researchers compared their results with those of 11 other studies and found a general agreement about the extent of genetic influence on schizophrenia, though there were methodological criticisms about the studies.

 Tip

You will study three 'studies in detail' for clinical psychology. One could be Gottesman and Shields (1966) as a study of schizophrenia. However, you will probably have chosen a different study for schizophrenia, as is done here. For the study that you need for each of the two research methods, make sure you know it also 'in detail', as questions on it could have depth.

Evaluation

Strengths

- Inouye (1961) in Japan found a 74% concordance rate for people with progressive chronic schizophrenia and 39% where twins had mild transient schizophrenia, so this study backs the finding of Gottesman and Shields (1966), which suggests reliability.
- There was careful sampling to make sure that the twins were accurately designated as MZ or DZ, which other studies had perhaps not done carefully enough, and also there was a lot of data gathered to check the diagnoses.

Weaknesses

- It would be useful to know more about what 'related psychosis' meant, as well as 'some other abnormality', as the researchers scaled the 'schizophrenia' diagnosis to take into account other abnormalities.
- Gottesman and Shields (1966) suggested that there are types of schizophrenia and some might come from life experiences, such as being a prisoner of war, but in the results it was hard to distinguish such different types.

Tip

This study is a twin study so you can use evaluation points for twin studies here as well as the above evaluation points, and you can use this example of a twin study when discussing twin studies as a research method.

Interviewing to study schizophrenia

Interviewing has been used to gather data about schizophrenia. For example, Gottesman and Shields (1966) used semi-structured interviewing with participants to find out about their mental functioning. There are three types of interview:

- Structured interviews are like questionnaires where there are set questions, though these can involve both open and closed questions. The difference from a questionnaire is that someone asks the questions and records the answers directly.
- Unstructured interviews have a schedule to list areas that need to be covered, but the actual questions are not set and the structure of the interview is free-flowing so that the interviewer can follow the thoughts of the interviewee and can note down more varied responses.

- Semi-structured interviews are a mix of the other two. There are set questions to be answered but the interviewer also has some freedom to ask other questions and explore the respondent's views in more depth.

Evaluation

Strengths
- Unstructured interviews tend to be valid because they allow the interviewer to explore issues that the respondent leads on, so there will be focus on what the interviewee wants to reveal.
- Interviews will gather qualitative data as well (in almost all cases), which means there is depth and detail which a more structured or controlled method will not provide.

Weaknesses
- There might be **interviewer bias** if the interviewer's dress or manner affects the replies. The way the questions are asked can also bias the responses.
- Detailed interview data can be analysed by looking for themes. This process can be subjective. For example, if Gottesman and Shields (1966) knew about a diagnosis for a participant, they may have inadvertently recorded data that matched that diagnosis.

Tip

Review your AS material on interviews, which you will have covered for the social approach. You may also have looked at interviewing as a method if you studied sport psychology.

Goldstein (1988)

You need to know a study using interviewing to look at schizophrenia. You could use Gottesman and Shields (1966) as they used semi-structured interviews. However, their study did not give much detail about the actual interviews (though there is some and more than has been given above), so it would be better to choose a study where the principal method used was interviewing. Goldstein (1988) is suggested in your course as a 'study in detail' and so is the one chosen here. As it is explained in depth in this section, it is not repeated again later. (Brown et al. (1986) also used interviewing to study unipolar depression: see pp. 61–62.)

Aims

Goldstein wanted to look at the differences in how males and females experience schizophrenia. She wanted to see if females experienced a less severe course of the illness than males. She had another aim, which was to see if DSM-III gave a different diagnosis from DSM-II. (You will read more about the DSM in the next section: see pp. 31–33.) She also looked at what factors besides gender affect the course of schizophrenia, such as past experience and environments (known as **premorbid history**).

Procedure

- Goldstein and others diagnosed 90 patients from a New York psychiatric hospital to check a diagnosis of schizophrenia. She used trained interviewers to go through symptoms and check them. She also used the case histories from the hospital.
- Using interviewing, she found out about past experiences, age, gender, ethnicity, class, marital status, level of education and level of social functioning.
- She also found out the number of rehospitalisations and the lengths of each stay in hospital — this was secondary data.
- She looked at gender against number of rehospitalisations, and gender against lengths of stay in hospital.
- She also looked at gender against those two features (rehospitalisations and lengths of stay) and other factors such as social functioning and premorbid history.

Results

- Goldstein (1988) found that women with schizophrenia did have a less severe course of the illness than men. Women had fewer rehospitalisations and shorter lengths of stay.
- Premorbid history affected the rehospitalisations more than they affected the length of a stay.
- Social functioning affected lengths of stay more than the number of rehospitalisations.

Conclusions

- Goldstein (1988) concluded that her study reinforced what other studies had found, supporting the hypothesis that women have a less severe course of schizophrenia than men.
- She also found that DSM-III was a reliable tool for diagnosis, but that there were some differences between DSM-II and DSM-III.
- She found that both social functioning and premorbid history were important features of schizophrenia.

Use Goldstein's findings about the reliability of the DSM when evaluating reliability of diagnosis, which is part of the content of your course.

Evaluation

Strengths

- The secondary data used, such as number of rehospitalisations and lengths of stay, are factual and objective data, so scientific conclusions can be drawn.
- Goldstein could show her diagnoses using DSM-III were reliable because she asked two experts to check them.
- By using interviewing she was able to gather in-depth qualitative data, so that information about premorbid history and social functioning (and other factors) was detailed.

Weaknesses
- Of women diagnosed with schizophrenia, 9% are over the age of 45, yet none in Goldstein's sample was over 45. Women over 45 seem to have a more severe form of schizophrenia — the statistics for women over 45 do not apply to men. So the findings might not be valid as the sample (of women) was limited.
- Goldstein used mainly white middle-class patients from one area in the USA and the sample was quite small, so perhaps the findings cannot be generalised to all schizophrenic patients.
- There might have been interviewer bias (p. 25).

Content

The content you need to cover includes two definitions of abnormality; the DSM classification system, and issues of reliability, validity and culture which arise in the diagnosis of abnormality; and two mental disorders, schizophrenia and one other disorder. Here, unipolar depression has been chosen as the second disorder. For both mental disorders you have to look at symptoms and features, explanations and treatments. Finally, you need to have covered one treatment for each of the five AS approaches, but those you covered for the two mental disorders can count.

Two definitions of abnormality

You need to be able to define and evaluate both the statistical deviation definition of abnormality and the social norm definition of abnormality.

Abnormality as deviation from statistical norms

This definition suggests that anything infrequent is abnormal. Anybody whose behaviour differs from the norm (i.e. is outside the middle range called 'normal') is called 'abnormal'. The middle is likely to be where the median, mean and modal scores are very similar. So when a score gets quite far away from the mean and other averages, then it is abnormal.

For example, if someone has a very low IQ they can be treated as abnormal and may be given additional help in society. In statistical terms they are likely to fall in the bottom two standard deviation bands, which in IQ terms means a score of 70 and below. Another example is that people do not 'normally' hear voices — such a characteristic is statistically infrequent so is labelled 'abnormal'. This definition involves statistical frequency — what is 'normal' means what is found most often and in most people.

A normal distribution curve has 95.4% of the scores either side of the mean within two standard deviation points. This is a high percentage and would be considered, therefore, statistically frequent. Any score outside that percentage (95.4%) would be considered statistically infrequent and, therefore, abnormal. Those that are

'abnormal' using this definition are those whose scores are the remaining 2.2% either side of the mean. (The percentages — 95.4, 2.2 and 2.2 — don't quite add up due to rounding but are close enough.)

The graph below helps to explain this. As IQ has a standard deviation of 15 and the mean is 100, you can tell that 70 is the IQ score at two standard deviation points away from the mean to the left of the graph, and 130 is the IQ score at two standard deviation points away from the mean to the right of the graph. Anyone with a score of under 70 or over 130 is thought of as abnormal — they fall within 2.2% of the population at the 'bottom' and 2.2% of the population at the 'top', so you can see this does seem logical, as that score would be statistically infrequent.

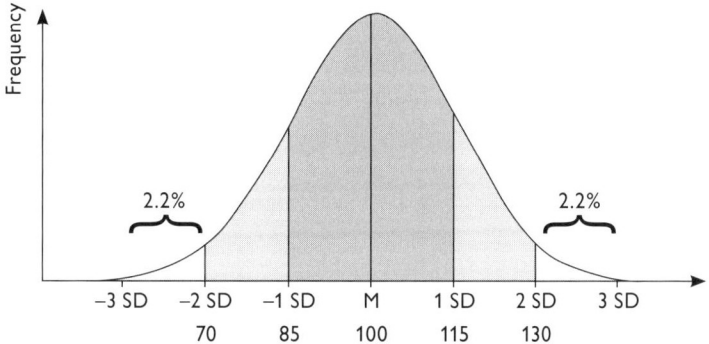

The DASS score

IQ at the 'low' end can be an example of a mental disorder but would not always be linked to clinical psychology. You can use it as an example because it works well to explain the definition. An example of a clinical score is the DASS score. This is the depression, anxiety and stress scale. A questionnaire is used which measures depression, anxiety and stress and helps to see how distressed someone is. The score should be quite low, up to 5 for each of the three areas measured. However, sometimes scores of 30 are found for each of the three areas for the same person. At this stage they would be considered distressed enough to be outside the 'norm' for the population — the DASS is used for diagnosis in this way. There would not be a low DASS score that is of concern, as there is in IQ. However, this is a measure where at one end of the scale there is concern, and where a high score is statistically infrequent and so taken as abnormal.

Evaluation

Strengths
- We can decide on a division to separate normal from abnormal. For example, an IQ score at the lower end (e.g. 70) could be the defining line between normal and abnormal. This means abnormality is easy to 'diagnose'. There is also an objective measure, which can help with funding.

- There is also a quantitative score and a test that can be repeated so data are likely to be reliable.

Weaknesses

- People with very high IQ scores, for example, are not normal in that they fall outside the middle range, but we would probably not say they were abnormal in the sense of being mentally ill. This is the same with a DASS score where a low score means mentally health.
- Having a single cut-off point presents difficulties. Who decides where that line lies? For example, if 70 IQ points is the cut-off, how can we justify saying that someone with 69 is abnormal, and someone with 70 is normal?
- One score may not be enough to define someone as abnormal. It may be necessary to look at more than one measure and not, for example, IQ alone.
- Abnormal behaviour is not rare and most people are likely to show abnormal (atypical) behaviour at some time in their lives. Depression is, in fact, quite common statistically.

Abnormality as deviation from social norms

The social norm definition of abnormality defines abnormality as unusual social behaviour. Someone might behave abnormally by showing strange, obsessive behaviour or violating social norms, such as wearing nightclothes in the street.

It might be that such unusual behaviour is statistically infrequent, which in a way you would expect, given that people do in general conform to social norms. However, the behaviour might be quite frequent in a society, though against social norms — so it is not the statistical infrequency that is the focus, but the violation of norms. For example, feeling depressed most of the time and not being able to get dressed or go out of the house is behaviour that (sadly) happens quite frequently in society, but it goes against social norms and what would be thought of in society as 'normal'.

This definition means that in different cultures different behaviours and characteristics are likely to be 'abnormal'. For example, hearing voices in one culture may be seen as part of being connected to spirits and normal in some sense, whereas in another society it may be seen as a main symptom of schizophrenia.

The context is also important because behaviour that would be against social norms in one situation might be seen as normal in another. For example, wearing a chicken suit in public might be seen as normal if done for an advertising campaign, but as abnormal if always done when out shopping. Historic context is also important — what was seen as normal years ago might be seen as abnormal now. It is amazing to think that someone who got pregnant outside marriage was sent to an institution around 100 years ago, but this did happen.

Evaluation

Strengths

- We tend to think of abnormality as involving odd behaviour, so this definition has appeal. Those with mental health problems do break social norms fairly often. This definition allows for someone very intelligent not to be seen as abnormal (unlike the statistically infrequent definition).
- This definition explains why different cultures can have different ideas about what is abnormal.

Weaknesses

- There may need to be several examples of antisocial behaviour before we are willing to label someone as 'abnormal' in the sense of mentally ill. Perhaps wearing nightclothes in the street and singing suggests abnormality more strongly than just wearing nightclothes, which you might do in an emergency.
- Criminals violate social norms but are not usually thought of as being mentally ill.
- Some people might be mentally ill, perhaps suffering from intense anxiety, but they might not break social norms.
- There are cultural differences in social norms, so measuring abnormality by means of such norms, which are not fixed, is unlikely to be useful.

Abnormality as dysfunction and distress (to evaluate)

You could use another definition to show the limitations of the two definitions you need to cover (statistical infrequency and breaking social norms). One way to define abnormality is to see if the behaviour is causing a problem for the person concerned. For example, people can have a fear of something yet only be diagnosed as having a phobia if that fear is preventing them from functioning in some way. If people cannot work because of their fear, then that is dysfunctional — it is interrupting their normal functioning and distressing them.

Evaluation

Strengths

- This definition is quite easy to apply as it is usually obvious when something is causing a problem. For example, it is dysfunctional for people if they cannot go out or go to work.
- It does take into account issues such as social functioning and premorbid factors as well as environmental triggers — all issues that have been mentioned already as being linked to mental illnesses. For example, life stressors can make someone distressed and unhappy, which can lead to depression or anxiety as well as a dysfunctional behaviour pattern.

Weaknesses

- However, what one person thinks of as abnormal and dysfunctional, such as not going out, someone else might consider quite normal. There is an element of subjectivity in the judgement.

- Psychopaths may need diagnosing, but may not be suffering any distress, and may be functioning normally as far as others can see.
- It is hard to measure distress, as this is subjective and experiences differ between individuals.

The DSM classification system

The DSM is the Diagnostic and Statistical Manual of Mental Disorders and is published by the American Psychological Association (APA). The most recent version is DSM-IV-TR. DSM-V is expected shortly. You could check on the internet to monitor its progress.

There are other classification systems, but it is the DSM that you need to know about. Doctors use the DSM to diagnose mental illness. It contains lists of symptoms that the patient's symptoms are matched to, with the best match being the diagnosis. Another system, the International Classification of Diseases (ICD), is published by the World Health Organization (WHO) and used across the world. ICD-10 was published in 1993. However, DSM is used widely, partly because many books on clinical psychology and diagnosis are American in origin.

Description of the DSM

The DSM looks at the pattern of symptoms, including the distress the person is experiencing. It uses a definition of abnormality linked to distress of the person and dysfunctioning (p. 30); it is not just a list of physical symptoms. Someone simply behaving in a way contrary to social norms would not be considered abnormal (pp. 29–30), and neither would someone who behaves abnormally 'statistically' (pp. 27–29). You could use information about the DSM to evaluate the two definitions of abnormality that you have to know about (for example by showing that they are not enough).

DSM-IV is a multi-axial system, which means it looks at patterns across different dimensions; there are five axes.

The five axes
For DSM-IV the five axes are as follows.
- Axis I — any clinical disorder or condition already present, other than personality disorders and mental retardation, including:
  - disorders usually first diagnosed in infancy, childhood or adolescence
  - substance-related disorders
  - schizophrenia/psychotic disorders
  - mood disorders
- Axis II — personality disorders, mental retardation, and other conditions (e.g. problems relating to abuse or neglect)
- Axis III — other general medical conditions that may affect diagnosis
- Axis IV — psychosocial and/or environmental problems that may affect diagnosis (such as family, educational, housing and economic problems)

- Axis V — Global Assessment of Functioning (GAF), which looks at psychological, social and occupational functioning along a continuum of mental illness to mental health (e.g. from 0 to 100, with 10 indicating someone in (persistent) danger of hurting themselves and 90 indicating minimal symptoms, such as anxiety before an exam)

Using the DSM in diagnosis

To diagnose, the clinician considers all five axes. Someone might be involved in substance abuse (Axis I), have a personality disorder (Axis II), have no other medical problems (Axis III), have educational problems (Axis IV) and be at risk of self-harm (Axis V). One of these would be the diagnosis, possibly the personality disorder. As you can see, having one problem is not enough for diagnosis, although in practice having a severe eating disorder, for example, is likely to lead to a low rating on the Global Assessment of Functioning scale (Axis V).

Evaluation of the DSM and its use

Strengths
- Costa and McCrae (1992) developed the Five-Factor Model of Personality (FFM), which considers neuroticism, agreeableness, conscientiousness, extroversion and openness to be the basic dimensions of personality. These dimensions have been used to diagnose personality disorders. It has been found that diagnoses based on the FFM correlate with those using Axis II of the DSM, which gives it reliability.
- Goldstein (1988) (pp. 25–27) found that the DSM-III was reliable, which is evidence for it being a useful diagnostic tool.
- The DSM has many specifics to try to ensure reliability and consistency. Reliability of diagnosis means that one person will receive the same diagnosis from different clinicians. Likewise, they will receive the same diagnosis if they go back to the same clinician at a different time with the same symptoms. Specific lists help to ensure reliability, but have their limitations (as discussed below).
- Validity of the DSM is also supported by having specific categories and examples in the manual. It is achieved when something measures what it claims to measure. For example, if you are diagnosed as having schizophrenia and you really do have it, there is validity, and treatments for schizophrenia can be expected to work. Validity is important because if you are diagnosed wrongly, you might receive the wrong treatment. DSM-IV, with its greater detail, is supposed to have improved reliability and validity.

Weaknesses
- Categorising is a limiting process because mental illness does not fall into categories so much as being along a continuum. We do not tend to be mentally ill or mentally healthy, but somewhere in between. This can be the case on different days, in different places, on different occasions. Diagnosing is not as straightforward as putting people into categories, which is what a classification system does.

- What counts as an illness changes over time. For example, homosexuality used to be in the manual, whereas it is not now considered a mental illness. However, if homosexuality is affecting someone, in that perhaps they wish to change their sexuality, then it can be diagnosed under a heading such as 'sexual disorder not otherwise specified'.

Advantages of being diagnosed

It might be thought that there is nothing to be gained from being diagnosed (labelled) as having a particular mental illness (or group of illnesses). You may have studied labelling and the effect of a self-fulfilling prophecy, and seen how it can be detrimental to someone. However, there are advantages to having a 'label':
- Financial help can be given in the form of allowances and support.
- In theory, any treatment offered should be suitable. A wrong diagnosis is likely to lead to the wrong treatment.
- Research can be carried out more easily, as people will have been grouped by their diagnosis, so can be grouped for the purposes of study. This might yield more information about the cause of the disorder, or more ideas concerning treatments and therapies, which can be advantageous to the individual.

Reliability issues in the diagnosis of disorders

Reliability means that if something is done again, the same results are found. If more than one psychologist gives the same diagnosis for the same set of symptoms (for the same person), then that diagnosis is considered reliable. Reliability would also be found if the same psychologist, on being presented with the same set of symptoms (for the same person) on a different occasion, gave the same diagnosis again.

However, psychologists can give different diagnoses for the same set of symptoms (which means diagnosis is unreliable). If diagnosis is unreliable, then treatment is possibly going to be incorrect and not helpful. The treatment could be bad for the patient, who might miss out on relief from more appropriate therapy.

Evaluation of reliability of diagnosis

Strengths
- Meehl (1977) argued that if all the categories are considered, and information is complete, then diagnosis can be reliable.
- Goldstein (1988) used a single blind technique, which means that she and other experts diagnosed the same participants separately. She used 190 participants who already had a diagnosis of schizophrenia. There was a lot of agreement between the diagnoses of the experts, which strongly suggests that DMS-III is reliable.
- Brown et al. (2001) used interviewing to test the diagnosis of anxiety and mood disorders in 362 outpatients in Boston, USA. Two independent interviews were carried out, using the anxiety disorders interview schedule for DSM-IV, and excellent reliability was found.

Weaknesses
- Beck et al. (1961) gave two psychiatrists the same 153 patients to diagnose and they agreed only 54% of the time. This suggests that diagnosis is not reliable.
- Unstructured interviews are not reliable and are often used. There is a schedule but the questions tend to be led by the interviewee and so the course of different interviews might be different and the results not comparable, so reliability cannot be tested for.
- A problem with the DSM is that there are not only symptoms but other issues such as how long they have lasted for and how severe they are. These issues can be subjectively judged and this can threaten reliability of diagnosis.
- Some disorders are at the boundaries of different disorders, such as generalised anxiety disorder, and they can be very hard to diagnose as symptoms can apply to different disorders.

Validity issues in the diagnosis of disorders

A diagnosis must be valid — it must measure what it is supposed to measure. If a diagnosis predicts the course of the illness and the symptoms, it is useful. It is also useful if it leads to the right treatment and the treatment works.

The classification system must lead to the diagnosis of the right illness. If the DSM is not reliable (though a lot of evidence suggests that it is) then it is not valid either, as if a different diagnosis is given at different times or by different doctors then the DSM cannot be measuring what it claims to measure.

A feature of diagnosis is that disorders have to be operationalised and categorised. It is possible that such categorisation is not suitable for mental health disorders, which tend to have complex symptoms and features. For example, depression is hard to diagnose — using a list of symptoms might not take into account the whole experience of depression, so the diagnosis might lack validity. This would be a lack of construct validity — the constructs drawn up in this case to represent depression are not representative enough.

Also, although the DSM now takes into account personal and social factors and how the person is functioning, these factors might not link to the mental disorder. For example, someone might be diagnosed with depression partly based on their social functioning, whereas that might come from some other cause such as unemployment. Then the diagnosis of depression might not be valid.

It has been argued that some categories of disorder ought not to be in the list, such as female hypoactive sexual desire disorder (low sex drive), which many would say is not a mental disorder. Another example is epilepsy, which used to be listed as a mental disorder, but is not now. Such examples suggest a lack of validity in having a diagnostic manual.

Etiological, concurrent and predictive validity
Etiological validity is found when a diagnosed problem is said to have the same cause for all those diagnosed with it. For example, if we say that bipolar disorder

(manic depression) has a genetic cause, then all sufferers should have a history of it somewhere in their family.

Concurrent validity is when other symptoms or factors found in one person, but not seen as part of the diagnosis, are also found in others with the same diagnosis. This would apply, for example, if all those with schizophrenia were found to have problems relating to others (which is not itself part of the diagnosis).

Predictive validity is found when those with a particular diagnosis follow the same future path — the course of the illness is the same. This means that at a later time, the person would be diagnosed with the same disorder, using a different way of measuring it.

Evaluation of validity of diagnosis

Strengths
- Kim-Cohen et al. (2005) used interviewing, questionnaires, observations and self-report data (and other means) to diagnose children with conduct disorder. They found that the different measures arrived at similar diagnoses; and when the children said to have conduct disorder were compared with peers, they were the children whose behaviour was disruptive. Their aim was to test the validity of the DSM-IV with regard to conduct disorder, as they used its measures. It was concluded that diagnosis is valid.
- Lee (2006) used a questionnaire with primary school teachers to see if questionnaire data matched the DSM-IV-TR criteria for ADHD (attention deficit hyperactivity disorder). They found that there was validity, as the teachers' questionnaire responses about children's behaviour matched the DSM criteria.
- As the above studies looked at conduct disorder and ADHD — different disorders — and both found the DSM to be valid, this strengthens the claim that overall the DSM has validity. There have been other studies as well.
- Studies have shown that the DSM is reliable, as discussed above, and it cannot be valid without being reliable — so when studies find that it is both reliable and valid, both claims are strengthened.

Weaknesses
- Some mental disorders are hard to diagnose. For example, manic depression is difficult to diagnose and is often misdiagnosed as schizophrenia or depression in the first instance.
- Symptoms often apply to various illnesses, so problems with diagnosis can occur. For example, paranoia can represent schizophrenia or substance abuse.
- If it were the case that one symptom represented one illness, there would perhaps be few problems. However, people are different, and although each illness might have a recognisable pattern, it is often not exactly the same for each person — so predictive validity is in doubt.
- There is co-morbidity, which is where someone has more than one mental disorder, and the DSM is not set up to deal with this easily because it relies on the clinician choosing the disorder that matches the symptoms most closely.

Tip

There is a lot of material here, and both validity and reliability issues with the DSM are involved in evaluating it. You could perhaps learn a definition for each, two points showing what the problem is in each case, two studies for each, two strengths and two weaknesses, if it is hard to learn more.

Cultural factors affecting the diagnosis of disorders

- Cultural factors create problems with diagnosis and are a source of bias. Cultural and subcultural (within-culture) differences, rather than an illness, may be the cause of problems, but these differences may not be recognised within that culture and a problem may be diagnosed as one of mental health.
- A classification system used in one culture might not be appropriate in another. Davison and Neale (1994) give an example, and explain how not expressing emotions might be normal in one culture but seen as a symptom of mental illness in another.
- Sabin (1975) reminds us that language difficulties and differences might mean misleading translation of symptoms, which could lead to misdiagnosis. Patients from one culture may not confide in clinicians from another culture.
- Such factors mean that mental illnesses are likely to be over-diagnosed for certain sections of the population. One example, given by Malgady et al. (1987), is the belief held by some Puerto Ricans that people can become possessed by evil spirits. If people from that culture talk about being possessed, it does not mean they are schizophrenic, but they might be diagnosed as such if their culture is not taken into account. Note that not all Hispanic peoples have this 'evil spirits' belief, so stereotyping can easily occur, also leading to misdiagnosis.
- In China, illness is seen as involving the balance (or imbalance) between yin and yang. Treatments reflect this belief, as would a Chinese classification system. This underlines the importance of taking beliefs and customs into account when diagnosing mental illness.
- There might be cultural differences in the course of a mental disorder. For example, it is thought that the catatonic form of schizophrenia is on the decline, possibly because of health measures. The evidence includes Chandrasena (1986), reporting a 21% incidence of catatonia in Sri Lanka compared with 5% among British white people. It was also found that there was less early intervention with drug treatment in Sri Lanka, which could have caused the difference.
- More auditory hallucinations are reported by doctors in Mexican-born Americans than in non-Mexican-born Americans (Burnham et al. 1987), with no explanation found except cultural differences.
- It is thought that there is more likely to be over-diagnosis in this country than under-diagnosis. For example, more West Indians in Britain are diagnosed as having mental illness than any other group, and this is likely to be due to misunderstanding of cultural issues.

Evaluation of claims of cultural bias in diagnosis

Strengths

'Strengths' here are points supporting the importance of bias and its potential negative effects for the person involved.

- Blake (1973) found that in the USA, African Americans are more likely to be diagnosed as schizophrenic than white Americans, which reflects the British findings, and suggests cultural bias in diagnosis.
- Malgady et al. (1987) give evidence for how cultural factors can bias diagnosis, as explained above.
- The DSM-IV-TR takes cultural issues into account when acknowledging culture-bound syndromes. These are syndromes such as kuru, which is an incurable brain disease found in Papua New Guinea. It is not a mental disorder but the symptoms are similar (it is like Creutzfeldt–Jakob disease and may come from the funeral practice of eating the brain). It is important that such a disease is not diagnosed as a mental disorder (for reliability and validity reasons), and in this way possible cultural bias is avoided.

Weaknesses

Here 'weaknesses' are points suggesting that the harmful effects of bias have been exaggerated.

- Lopez (1989) suggests that if we are too careful to take culture and beliefs into account, we may under-diagnose a particular illness. If people are not diagnosed as being schizophrenic, for example, because it is thought that they are hearing voices as part of their belief system, then they may miss out on necessary treatment (if they actually have schizophrenia).
- Chandrasena (1986) found that it was not the culture itself that was the important factor so much as different cultural practices such as those concerning health care, as explained above.

Overcoming cultural bias, and validity and reliability concerns

- One way to help overcome cultural bias is to focus more on symptoms and features that are likely to be universal and not on those that might be different in different cultures. For example, there should be less focus on bizarre behaviour (as 'bizarreness' is a judgement) and more on difficulties with social functioning or distress.
- Flaum (1991) suggested that negative symptoms of schizophrenia are more objectively measured than positive ones (like hallucinations) and so should be focused on more.
- The DSM has been revised many times and each time issues such as culture, validity and reliability are considered. For example, global functioning was focused on so that diagnosis was not just about a list of symptoms. By having the five axes it was thought that validity and reliability would be improved.
- When DSM-IV was reviewed and became DSM-IV-TR (in 2000), removing 'bizarre' was considered but it was thought that 'bizarreness' was too important a feature

of schizophrenia. However, a warning was added about the need to consider that 'bizarre' is a judgement and could entail cultural differences.

You might get a question about how to improve validity and reliability in diagnosis, or a question about how to avoid cultural bias in diagnosis. Be prepared to use your material in this way.

Schizophrenia

The following sections look at symptoms and features of schizophrenia, two explanations for schizophrenia and two treatments for schizophrenia.

Symptoms and features of schizophrenia

Schizophrenia is a psychosis, which means that the individual does not have the grip on reality that someone suffering from a neurosis has. Symptoms of schizophrenia include hallucinations, thought disorders, language disturbances and inappropriate feelings (or flattening of feelings).

There are five different types of schizophrenia. The different types are characterised by different symptoms. For example, catatonic schizophrenia involves immobility or excessive motor activity (or some rigidity of posture), whereas these might not occur in other types of schizophrenia. Indeed, the diagnosis of the type of schizophrenia is made by reference to such symptoms, so it is hard to make a list of symptoms of schizophrenia without referring to the different types. Two of the types are catatonic schizophrenia (where someone is withdrawn and isolated, with a disordered pattern of movement such as immobility) and paranoid schizophrenia (where someone is suspicious of others and has delusions of grandeur, for example).

Around 1% of the population has schizophrenia and this statistic is more or less the same across all cultures. This might suggest an element of genetic cause — if it were environmental, one might expect different levels of schizophrenia in different cultures (this could link to the nature–nurture debate, pp. 86–87).

There are some gender differences (again possibly suggesting a genetic cause). Men tend to exhibit symptoms sooner, usually between 14 and 25 years of age, whereas women show symptoms between about 24 and 35 years of age.

With five different types, and many varying symptoms that in some ways contradict (e.g. withdrawal versus excessive excitability, or rigidity of posture versus excessive movement), it might be suggested that 'schizophrenia' is only a term used to cover a range of 'odd' or abnormal behaviours. Perhaps it is not 'one thing' at all. In this case it would not have one cause either.

Some of the above information suggests that there is a genetic element to schizophrenia. This would be useful evidence if you were discussing the nature–nurture debate. If it is argued that there are many types of schizophrenia, probably some types or some parts of it are inherited and other parts or types come about through environmental pressures.

Positive symptoms

Sometimes symptoms of schizophrenia are split into positive and negative ones. Positive symptoms are seen when someone with schizophrenia exhibits behaviours that are not 'normal'. Negative symptoms are noted when a schizophrenic fails to exhibit 'normal' behaviours.

Positive symptoms include:
- Disorganised speech, including loose association/derailment. Loose association occurs when someone changes from one topic to another during speech, with no connection between the topics: for example, 'It's all part of the family, you know, those who are in and the ones who never get to see the words' (Kendall and Hammen, 1995).

  Evaluation: Andreason (1979) says that other disorders, such as mania, can also show loose associations and that not all of those with schizophrenia have disorganised speech.
- Delusions — thoughts which most of society would disagree with, or which are misinterpretations of reality, e.g. the belief that others are plotting against you. Delusions are found in 50% of schizophrenic patients, but also occur in mania and delusional depression. There are several different types of delusion, including somatic passivity (where someone believes they are receiving bodily sensations from another agency) and thought insertion (where someone believes that thoughts not their own are being placed in their mind).
- Hallucinations — experiences where the world seems unreal, the body seems depersonalised and the person has odd sensations such as burning or numbness. Individuals can experience acute perceptions, such as very bright light or clear colours. On the other hand, they can experience a flattening or dullness. Hallucinations are sensory experiences in the absence of any stimulation from the environment and involve mainly auditory perceptions (sounds). In schizophrenia, hallucinations often involve hearing voices arguing or voices commenting.

Negative symptoms

Negative symptoms include:
- Avolition/apathy, which is characterised by a lack of energy and an absence of interest, even in routine. For example, a person may not brush his or her hair and may have dishevelled clothing.
- Alogia, which refers to negative thought disorder. There is poverty of speech, and also poor content of speech, giving little information.
- Anhedonia, which is an inability to experience pleasure. There is a lack of interest in recreational activities and no relationships are formed.
- Flat affect, which means that an individual exhibits no emotions. It is found in 66% of schizophrenics, according to an International Pilot Study of Schizophrenia (IPSS) survey in 1974.

Evaluation: The person may experience emotions inside, but not show them. Kring (1990) compared schizophrenics with flat affect with normal participants when watching a film, and the schizophrenics showed no emotions. However, when asked about the film afterwards, the individuals with flat affect reported the same emotions — they just had not shown them.

Other symptoms

The following symptoms are neither positive nor negative:

- Catatonia, which involves disturbances in movement patterns. There may be a tendency to adopt strange facial expressions or to gesture repeatedly. Some people move much more than usual and show excited movements. Others are immobile and unusual positions are adopted for quite a long time.
- Inappropriate affect, which is when someone shows the wrong emotional responses to a situation.

Make sure that you note the difference between symptoms and features. Most of the information here is about symptoms, but there are features as well — such as that around 1% of the population is affected by schizophrenia and that there are different types of schizophrenia. Questions can focus on symptoms, features or both.

Explanations for schizophrenia

This section focuses mainly on two explanations for schizophrenia, though there are others. You need to cover two explanations, including a biological one. The two focused on here are the dopamine hypothesis, a biological explanation, and the social class 'environmental breeder' hypothesis, a social explanation.

First, however, the genetic explanation (the other main biological explanation) is briefly outlined. This is included because it relates to the use of twin studies and might be useful when discussing them (pp. 21–24) (as well as Gottesman's work). This material will also be useful when you study the nature–nurture debate for the Issues and Debates section of the course (pp. 86–87).

You may have covered explanations other than the two focused on here, in which case you might prefer to revise them.

The genetic explanation for schizophrenia: one biological explanation

Twin and adoption studies suggest that there is an element of heritability to schizophrenia.

Evidence from twin studies

- Gottesman found that identical (MZ) twins have a 48% risk factor (if one twin has it, there is a 48% likelihood that the other one will). Non-identical (DZ) twins have a 17% risk factor. The likelihood of developing schizophrenia for the whole population is 1%, so these findings strongly suggest a genetic factor.

- Torrey (1992) found lower figures than Gottesman's, but still 28% for identical twins and 6% for non-identical twins, which are higher than the 1% for the general population.
- McGue (1992) found a risk factor of 40% for identical twins.

Evidence from adoption studies

- It is found that an adopted child who develops schizophrenia is likely to have a biological parent with schizophrenia.
- An adopted child raised in a (non-biological) family where a member has schizophrenia is not so likely to develop it.
- Thus it seems that biological background, rather than an environment in which schizophrenia is present, leads to an individual developing schizophrenia.

Evaluation of the genetic explanation for schizophrenia

Strengths

- All three twin studies mentioned above found higher risk factors for twins than the 1% for the general population — this is quite strong evidence for a genetic cause (nature).
- The biological link for schizophrenia in families compared with the lack of environmental link — based on evidence from adoption studies — is quite compelling evidence.

Weaknesses

- The three different twin studies found different figures, which means evidence must be questioned.
- In the twin studies, twins (and relatives to an extent) share environment as well as genes, so the above percentages might be evidence that schizophrenia is environmentally caused (nurture).
- Schizophrenia may be linked to more than one gene, so it is hard to pin down a genetic cause.
- There seems to be more than one type of schizophrenia, so there may be more than one cause.
- If it was wholly caused by genetics, one MZ twin should automatically develop schizophrenia if the other one does, because MZ twins share 100% of their genes. However, this is not the case — even the highest estimate is just under 50%.

The above evaluation points will be useful in a discussion about nature–nurture, which is a debate you have to study for the Issues and Debates part of the course.

The dopamine hypothesis: another biological explanation for schizophrenia

- Neurochemical medication seems to help in relieving the symptoms of schizophrenia. This suggests that a neurotransmitter is the problem, or that there might be problems with synaptic transmission.
- Phenothiazine drugs reduce symptoms of schizophrenia. They block dopamine receptors, so schizophrenia may be due to an excess of dopamine, a neurotransmitter (and chemical). This is the dopamine hypothesis, a neurochemical explanation for schizophrenia.
- Drugs that increase dopamine activity (such as amphetamine) make the symptoms worse, which is added evidence for a neurochemical cause.
- It is possible that an increase in dopamine in the mesolimbic pathway in the brain contributes positive symptoms while an increase in dopamine in the mesocortical pathway in the brain contributes negative symptoms.
- Genetic inheritance might cause the sensitivity to dopamine, so the two explanations (genetic and neurochemical) could link.

Evaluation of the dopamine hypothesis to explain schizophrenia

Strengths

- Phenothiazines block dopamine receptors and alleviate the symptoms of schizophrenia. Blocking the receptors blocks excess dopamine, which suggests that excess dopamine is causing the symptoms.
- Amphetamines can cause excess dopamine and lead to symptoms of psychosis, symptoms which are similar to positive symptoms in schizophrenia.
- Scanning shows that when those with schizophrenia are given amphetamines, there is a greater release of dopamine than if non-schizophrenics are given amphetamines. This lends support to the idea that dopamine is involved in schizophrenia.

Weaknesses

- Not all those with schizophrenia respond to drug treatment, so it seems that not all cases of schizophrenia are caused by excess dopamine.
- Drugs work with some symptoms but not all — again suggesting that excess dopamine, even if part of the story for some, is not the whole story. More research is needed.
- The excess dopamine may be produced in response to the schizophrenia, rather than being a cause of it.
- Blocking dopamine does not work straight away, which suggests there is more to schizophrenia than excess dopamine.
- Amphetamines only produce positive symptoms, which suggests there is more to schizophrenia than excess dopamine. In addition, there are symptoms of mania when amphetamines are used, whereas such symptoms are not characteristic of schizophrenia.

Strengths and weaknesses of the methodology used to study the dopamine hypothesis

Strengths	Weaknesses
Many different sources of evidence point to dopamine receptors being involved in some way in schizophrenia, from animal studies to PET scanning. Evidence also comes from unrelated events, such as how medication affects those with Parkinson's disease or how using recreational drugs leads to psychotic symptoms.	Animals are used to investigate dopamine pathways and the effects of drugs on them. Lesioning is also used with animals to explore the effects of dopamine on their functioning. It is possible that findings from animal studies cannot legitimately be generalised to humans, because there are obvious differences in animal brains and the functioning of their nervous systems.
Dopamine receptors are implicated in many different studies, which tends to give the hypothesis reliability.	Scanning is carried out, which is a reliable and objective measure. However, there is a lack of sophistication so that detail is hard to study, even though functioning of the brain can be looked at.
'Biological' research methods such as scanning and animal studies can have good controls and tend not to involve subjective interpretation of data, so such methods are scientific, which means the findings are credible.	Something else to do with schizophrenia may have caused the differences in dopamine receptors, rather than dopamine receptor differences causing schizophrenia.

Tips

- Make sure you give one biological explanation and not two, if asked for one.
- For evaluation points you can use strengths and weaknesses of methodology — this links to the methodology section of this application, where you are asked to study two methods used to look at schizophrenia (and one study for each).

The 'environmental breeder' hypothesis: a social explanation for schizophrenia

General life stresses can lead to a relapse, so perhaps they are a cause of schizophrenia. Social class seems to be linked to the incidence of schizophrenia. It seems to be a factor which is somehow involved in causing schizophrenia or in its development.

In the UK, various studies have found a higher rate of schizophrenia diagnosis in the lower social classes (in both the white population and black immigrant population) than in other classes (e.g. Eaton et al. 1988, reporting on 17 studies). Schizophrenia is found regularly among the unemployed and those in deprived city areas. Lower-class patients are more likely to be brought for help by police or social services and to be compulsorily admitted. In the 1960s it was thought that lower class was a causal factor in schizophrenia and this was called the 'environmental breeder' hypothesis.

There are two social factors that have been considered in explanations: social drift, and environmental causation factors such as stress. As explained below, the social selection theory focuses on social drift, while the sociogenic hypothesis focuses on environmental factors like stress.

Social selection theory suggests that it is not that class causes schizophrenia but that those with the illness drift downwards in terms of class. They may earn less because of cognitive and motivational difficulties. This is **social drift**, where those with difficulties drift down the social classes. One study compared the social class of men with schizophrenia with that of their fathers, and found that the schizophrenic men were in the lower classes but their fathers generally were not. This suggested that the men had drifted downwards because of the schizophrenia. For example, they had had problems in adolescence and difficulties in getting a job. The idea of social drift is now widely accepted; nonetheless, an environmental cause for schizophrenia, as proposed by the sociogenic hypothesis, cannot be ruled out.

The **sociogenic hypothesis** focuses on stress factors associated with class. The highest rate of schizophrenia is in central city areas, which are inhabited by the lowest socioeconomic class (Srole et al. 1962). Eaton et al. (2000) suggest that, as there are more incidences of schizophrenia in cities than in rural areas, something in city life might lead to schizophrenia. In central city areas, the incidence of schizophrenia can be as much as double normal levels, so we can ask whether social class is in some way a cause of schizophrenia. The sociogenic hypothesis suggests that stress resulting from a low level of education, with poor rewards and opportunities, can lead to schizophrenia.

Evidence
- Hjem et al. (2004) showed in Sweden that social adversity in childhood related to the development of schizophrenia later.
- Census data (1991 and 2001) in the UK consistently show more African-Caribbean and black immigrants as having schizophrenia.
- Fearon et al. (2004) estimate four times more schizophrenia in the African-Caribbean and black immigrant population than in the white indigenous population, and black immigrants in lower classes could not have suffered from social drift.
- It is not likely that genes are responsible for the above differences in the black and white populations, because in Caribbean countries, for example, the incidence of schizophrenia is similar to the general rate in the UK for the indigenous population.

Tip

When making statements about social class relating to or causing schizophrenia, as with any other claims in psychology, remember to give some evidence for your claims.

Evaluation of the idea that environmental factors lead to schizophrenia

- There is conflicting evidence concerning social drift. Some studies, such as Schwartz (1946), show that schizophrenics are downwardly mobile, but other studies (e.g. Dunham 1965) show that they are not. One way of testing this is to see if fathers of those with schizophrenia are lower-class. If they are, it would show that schizophrenics were already members of the lower classes rather than having arrived there by downward mobility. If fathers are lower-class, this would support the sociogenic hypothesis — that those with schizophrenia are in the lower classes and the illness might be caused by stress and environmental factors.
- Dohrenwend et al. (1992) looked at ethnic minorities. If the sociogenic hypothesis is accepted then, because of prejudice and discrimination, with resultant stress, one would expect ethnic minority groups to have more incidents of schizophrenia across all classes though there would be more in the lower social classes, where stress might be greater. The rates are indeed higher in lower-class groups. This seems to be evidence for the influence of environmental factors related to class. The evidence does not back the idea of social drift, as immigrants tend to be in the lower classes more (of course this is all about generalisations and not about individuals).
- Studies have found that schizophrenia links to social class through more than 'just' social drift — such as Fearon et al.'s (2004) evidence that some groups are more affected by schizophrenia but could not have drifted down the classes (as they were not in higher classes in the first place).
- Tienari et al. (1987) carried out studies in Finland. They studied the environment of adopted children, some of whom had mothers with schizophrenia and some of whom did not. The more problematic the environment, the more severe were the problems that the children of schizophrenics had. A problematic environment did not, however, lead to problems in adopted children without a schizophrenic mother. It seems, therefore, that an element of genetic predisposition, as well as environmental influences, is involved in causing schizophrenia.
- There could be a diagnosis problem, with more in the lower classes being diagnosed as having schizophrenia, rather than more actually having schizophrenia.

 Tip

You studied the social approach for AS Unit 1. Recall now that its main assumptions focus on the importance of interactions between people, and how they affect what we do and what we are like. It also emphasises the importance of groups — in other words, that we do not act as individuals without influences from society around us.

Two treatments for schizophrenia

The two treatments chosen here are drug treatment (from the biological approach) and assertive community therapy (a psychosocial treatment, from the social approach)

Tip

You may have studied different treatments for schizophrenia and you might prefer to revise those instead of learning new ones.

Drug treatment for schizophrenia

Drugs used to treat schizophrenia are called 'antipsychotic' drugs and they work to suppress hallucinations and delusions. There are typical antipsychotic drugs, which are the well-established ones. Atypical antipsychotic drugs are newer, less widely used ones that tend to have fewer side-effects and work in different ways to typical ones.

An example of a typical antipsychotic drug used in the treatment of schizophrenia is chlorpromazine (first used in 1952 and a phenothiazine). Side-effects of typical antipsychotic drugs can include sleepiness, shaking, low blood pressure and weight gain.

Most drugs work at the synapse, either modelling or blocking a neurotransmitter. The effect is more activity of that neurotransmitter if modelled by the drug, or less activity as the work of that neurotransmitter is blocked by the drug.

Evaluation of drug treatment

Strengths
- Some might say that drug treatment is quick and easy for medical professionals, as well as more ethical than treatment before the 1950s.
- Meltzer et al. (2004) looked at the effectiveness of drug treatment for schizophrenia. There were 481 patients with schizophrenia; some were given a placebo, some an investigational new drug (there were four of these drugs, so different groups), and some haloperidol, an established antipsychotic drug. They found that haloperidol was effective compared with the placebo drug, as were two of the new drugs. This is evidence that drug treatment works at least to an extent.
- Drug treatment rests on strong biological evidence (such as the dopamine hypothesis and evidence that schizophrenia is linked to neurotransmitter functioning) so is underpinned by theory.

Weaknesses
- It is possible that the use of drugs masks the problem but does not treat it. One symptom can simply replace another.
- Kane et al. (1988) found that between 10% and 20% of people do not improve if given drug therapy (although this presumably means that the others do improve in some way).
- Drugs may treat the symptoms, but it is doubtful if they address the cause of the disorder. Often the patient has to continue using the drugs, despite problems of dependence, tolerance and toxicity. Dependence can occur.
- Side-effects can be a problem. Drugs often act by mimicking or blocking neurotransmitter movements in some way. A neurotransmitter is likely to have many roles in the nervous system. The drug might help with some of the symptoms of the illness, but may also affect other functions of the nervous

system. Antipsychotic drugs, for example, can lead to tremors and jerking. Some drugs are toxic.

- It is thought that about 50% of those with schizophrenia stop taking the drugs they are prescribed, possibly because of the nature of the illness, which involves problems in functioning.

Tip

Drug treatment for unipolar depression is explained later in this section; you can use some of these evaluation points when discussing either schizophrenia or unipolar depression. As well, you will need to know a treatment for each of the five AS approaches, so you can use drug treatment as one of these and make use of the material you have learned here. You will need to talk about a contribution of the biological approach and a contribution of clinical psychology, and drug treatment is suitable for both those areas also. So this material can be used for a number of different questions in Unit 4.

Assertive community therapy for schizophrenia

Assertive community therapy (ACT) is a psychosocial treatment (from the social approach).

ACT is one 'care in the community' programme and helps schizophrenic patients who have frequent relapses and bouts of hospitalisation. Clients with problems meeting personal goals, making friends, and living independently are helped using ACT, which was developed by Leonard Stein, Mary Ann Test and others, in what was originally called the Madison Project.

There is a focus on those who need the most help, and on independence, rehabilitation and recovery to avoid homelessness and rehospitalisation. Treatment takes place in the real-life setting of the patient, where they are visited and helped. The programme involves many professionals, including psychiatrists, social workers, and nurses. The commitment is to spend as much time with the person as necessary to rehabilitate and support them, offering a holistic treatment based on a multidisciplinary approach.

Evaluation of Assertive Community Therapy (ACT)

Strengths
- Bond et al. (2001) summarised 25 controlled studies that looked at the effectiveness of ACT (which is known as an evidence-based treatment because there is evidence of its effectiveness). It was thought to be highly effective because it engages clients, prevents rehospitalisation, increases stability in a client's life and improves quality of life.
- Surveys tend to show that clients appreciate ACT (Mueser et al. 1998), which seems to work with all age groups, with both genders and in different cultures.
- The medical approach seems to ignore social factors that might be involved in the diagnosis of mental disorders. The social approach focuses on ethnic group, social class, environment and problems with living. This leads to more focus on prevention, which could be said to be better than 'cure'.

Weaknesses
- Gregory (2001) suggests that ACT is coercive in that the client does not have a choice about undergoing the treatment. About 11% appear to feel forced into the treatment (Bond 2002).
- The ideals behind care in the community programmes might be genuine, but social factors include political ones. There tends to be a problem when practical factors such as cost and number of health professionals available are confused with 'caring' reasons for decisions. Evaluation of programmes is often funded by government, and looks at issues such as cost and staffing, rather than focusing purely on how far a programme is successful in itself.
- There have been reported cases in which those who are mentally ill have failed to keep up with necessary medication and consequently have experienced problems. In these instances, it is said that community programmes have failed those in their care.
- ACT does not help with positive and negative symptoms, or with employment prospects, though it does help with some problems of living. Supportive employment programmes would also be needed.
- ACT works in a heavily populated area because there are enough clients to make it cost-effective, but it is costly with regard to staffing and time, so it may be limited to areas where it can be used effectively.

Unipolar depression

The following sections look at unipolar depression: symptoms and features first, followed by two explanations and finally two treatments.

Unipolar depression is also known as clinical depression, unipolar disorder or major depression. It is called unipolar depression to distinguish it from bipolar or manic depression, but here it will often be referred to as just 'depression', which is usual.

You may have studied a different 'second' mental disorder (as well as schizophrenia), so you may prefer to revise that rather than learn a new one.

Symptoms
- Symptoms include feelings of worthlessness and hopelessness, loss of sleep and appetite, guilt, sadness and loss of interest and pleasure in usual activities.
- For some sufferers, paying attention is difficult and conversation can be hard. Others find it hard to switch off and cannot sit still. Some develop hypochondria.
- When using the DSM, only some of these symptoms have to be present for the diagnosis to be made. For a diagnosis of unipolar disorder, there must be mood disturbances, loss of (or too much) sleep, loss (or gain) of weight, loss (or gain) of appetite and a disturbed activity level.
- DSM-IV says that there must be five symptoms from the list and that these must last for at least 2 weeks. Depressed mood and loss of pleasure or interest must be two of these five symptoms.

Features

- Symptoms change with age. Depression in children can mean aggression and a lot of activity, whereas in adolescents it is often characterised by antisocial behaviour and feelings of being misunderstood. In older adults, it leads to memory problems and distractibility.
- Phases of depression can last for up to 6 months.
- Unipolar depression tends to start between the ages of 30 and 40 and to peak between 50 and 60, and is more common in women and lower socioeconomic groups.
- Depression affects over 3.5 million people in the UK.

Explanations for unipolar disorder

This section focuses mainly on two explanations for unipolar depression: the monoamine hypothesis, a biological explanation involving neurochemicals; and the cognitive model of depression, a cognitive explanation. First, however, it looks very briefly at the role of genes in unipolar depression, in order to give a fuller picture. You only need to know two explanations and here it is suggested you learn the monoamine explanation from the biological approach and the cognitive explanation as your second one.

The role of genes in unipolar depression

Before looking at neurochemical factors in unipolar depression it is worth looking at the role of genes, so that you have a fuller picture of biological factors that might be at work. In unipolar disorders, genes do not play as strong a role as in bipolar disorders (manic depression). However, if there is a bipolar disorder in the family, there is quite a strong chance of a first-degree relative developing a mood disorder, which is often unipolar. This suggests that unipolar disorder could be genetic and linked to bipolar disorder.

Evaluation of a genetic component in unipolar depression

Strengths (evidence in favour)

- Andreason et al. (1987) point out that there is more risk of unipolar disorder developing in families with bipolar disorder than in families with unipolar disorder.
- Allen (1976) suggests a concordance rate of 40% for MZ twins and 11% for DZ twins, which suggests a genetic component for unipolar disorder.
- Adoption studies support the claim that genes are involved in depression. For example, Cadoret (1978) found that there were more mood disorders in adopted children where one of the biological parents had a mood disorder.

Weaknesses

- Although we can draw conclusions about genes from twin studies, we must not overlook the very similar environments and interactions that twins share. Even if we say that the rates for MZ twins are always higher than for DZ and that this proves the genetic element, we could counter this by claiming that there are closer similarities in the environments and treatments experienced by MZ twins.

- If depression were entirely genetic, an MZ twin would always develop a mood disorder when the other twin had one, and this is not the case.

The monoamine hypothesis: another biological explanation

- Monoamines are a group of neurotransmitters including serotonin, norepinephrine and dopamine.
- There is evidence to suggest that low levels of norepinephrine can cause depression and high levels can cause mania. This suggests that there is a biological basis for mood disorders such as unipolar and bipolar depression.
- Another neurotransmitter that might be involved is serotonin. Serotonin is often involved in neural activity involving other neurotransmitters. If serotonin levels are low, this could lead to problems in other neural activity and consequently to depression or mania.
- One role of serotonin is to regulate other transmitters and without regulation there can be erratic brain functioning and thinking patterns.
- Low levels of norepinephrine, which is needed for someone to be alert and have energy, can come from low levels of serotonin, another link to depression.
- Dopamine is related to the ability to show motivation and attention and to feel pleasure, so low levels of dopamine will link to depression.
- The idea of drug treatment (pp. 52–54) is to match the drug to the symptoms so that the particular monoamine concerned is increased.

Evaluation of the monoamine hypothesis

Strengths (evidence in favour)

- Evidence comes from the success of tricyclic drugs in alleviating depression. Tricyclic drugs interfere with the reuptake of norepinephrine and serotonin. This suggests a role for these neurotransmitters in causing depression, because the lack of reuptake might mean more of them being at the synapse rather than being used for typical functioning.
- Evidence also comes from the success of monamine oxidase inhibitors in alleviating depression. These drugs stop the enzyme monoamine oxidase from deactivating neurotransmitters. This will increase levels of serotonin and norepinephrine.
- Another piece of evidence is that reserpine, which is prescribed to calm those with schizophrenia, has led to some patients developing depression. Reserpine lowers levels of serotonin and norepinephrine, and this again is evidence that low levels of these neurotransmitters might cause depression.

Weaknesses

- It could be that the mood disorder led to the change in level of serotonin rather than the level causing the mood disorder.
- As research continues, the above findings are being contradicted. Tricyclics and monoamine oxidase inhibitors do seem to increase levels of norepinephrine and serotonin at first, but after a few days the norepinephrine levels go back to normal. As it takes more than a week for tricyclics and monoamine oxidase inhibitors to

work, and as by this time the neurotransmitter levels are back to normal, the idea that the low levels of these two neurotransmitters cause depression must be challenged.

- Other antidepressant drugs work (such as opipramol), but not by increasing levels of these two neurotransmitters; their action is not related to monoamine neurotransmitters (e.g. Cole 1986).
- Much of the research comes from animal studies and we must take care when generalising findings from animal studies to humans.
- A different biological explanation implicates the parts of the nervous system related to stress, and an increase in the levels of cortisol. This goes against the monoamine hypothesis.

 Tip

When mentioning an alternative explanation to show a weakness of a theory or explanation, only give this point once as there is likely to be only 1 mark there — otherwise you would be talking about the 'other explanation' and changing the question.

The cognitive model of depression: a cognitive explanation

Depression is an example of a disorder that can be explained by reference to principles within the cognitive approach. If depression involves negative thought patterns, as it seems to, then encouraging rebalancing of negative thoughts might be one way of helping someone to overcome depression.

Cognitive restructuring can be a good way of overcoming disorders such as depression. In cognitive–behavioural therapy, changing thought processes is believed to change behaviour and emotions (pp. 54–56).

Beck's cognitive model of depression

Depression is often characterised by negative thoughts, feelings of helplessness and irrational beliefs. Beck (1967, 1987) thought depression arose from negative interpretations of events. Individuals who become depressed develop negative schemata. This can be for reasons such as rejection by peers, loss of a parent, or criticism from teachers. These schemata are then triggered by new situations.

There are also cognitive biases, such as individuals thinking they will fail or feeling responsible for problems. There is a triad of negative views — of the self, the world and the future. Beck's model includes the cognitive triad, cognitive errors (faulty thinking and unrealistic ideas) and schemata (patterns of maladaptive thoughts and beliefs). The cognitive triad involves the depressed person having negative thoughts about themselves (feeling unworthy and inadequate), about the world (feeling deprived or defeated) and about the future (feeling that the suffering will continue).

Early experiences and genetic factors produce beliefs, which set up assumptions about the world — which can lead to negative automatic thoughts. Schemata involve developing positive and negative beliefs and attitudes to interpret the world. A pattern of negative beliefs can make someone vulnerable to depression. Likely schemata of someone who is depressed include cognitive schemata that lead to seeing loss,

emotion schemata that lead to sadness, biological schemata that make someone tired and not able to do things, motivational schemata that lead to helplessness, and behavioural schemata that lead to withdrawal and inactivity.

Evaluation of the cognitive model for depression

Evidence in favour

- Hollon et al. (2002) found that cognitive–behavioural therapy (CBT — a treatment that rests on the cognitive model and is explained later in this section) performed well in controlled trials. CBT helps at least as long as drug treatment.
- Bothwell and Scott (1997) found that faulty thinking and errors in cognitive processing are linked with symptoms of depression continuing after hospital care.
- Teichman et al. (2002) looked at relationships between self-concept, hostility between self and partner, a partner's level of depression, involvement in house activities and how severe depression was. They found that self-concept had the most marked link with the severity of the depression. This is evidence for the cognitive model of depression as self-concept involves how people see themselves and is an opinion.
- The model is evidence-based as there is evidence to support it — as shown here.
- Beck (1967) and White et al. (1992) showed that depressed people do have cognitive biases such as overgeneralising, mind-reading, and black and white thinking — some of the maladaptive ways of thinking that characterise depression.
- After treatment, biased thinking seems to disappear, according to Simons et al. (1984).

Weaknesses

- Other studies, such as Dykman et al. (1991), have not found such biases. Depressed people do not seem to have a distorted perception of their own abilities. Perhaps they do focus on the negative parts of events but they do perceive them accurately, which is a slightly different explanation.
- Perhaps the mood (being depressed) is what distorts perceptions, rather than the distorted perceptions causing the mood. Lewinsohn et al. (1981) found negative thinking did not come before depression, which suggests that depression causes the cognitive biases, not the other way around.

Two treatments for unipolar depression

This section looks at drug treatment for unipolar depression (from the biological approach) and cognitive–behavioural therapy or CBT (from the cognitive approach).

These treatments link to the explanations given above — it is useful to study the treatment that matches the explanation you have studied. If you have studied different treatments from the ones given here, you might prefer to revise them rather than learning something new.

Drug treatment for unipolar depression

Unipolar depression is often treated by drugs such as tricyclic antidepressants, monoamine oxidase inhibitors (MAOs), and selective serotonin reuptake inhibitors (SSRIs) such as Prozac.

The idea is that if the level of a neurotransmitter is low and causing depression, drugs could be used to raise the level of that neurotransmitter, such as serotonin or dopamine. For example, Prozac increases levels of serotonin and helps with depression — though that does not prove that low levels of serotonin are the cause of the depression. Tricyclic and atypical antidepressants target other neurotransmitters like norepinephrine and dopamine, as well as serotonin.

These drugs often work at the synapse where neurotransmitters are passing across from the axon of one neurone to the receptors of another neurone. Some drugs prevent reuptake: they leave the neurotransmitter to pass its signal via the receptors of the receiving neurone but inhibit the reuptake pumps which would remove it from the synaptic gap. Some drugs excite neuronal activity; some inhibit activity. All drugs have side-effects.

Kuyken et al. (2008) compared drug treatment and a form of CBT. They found that a group-based form of CBT was at least as successful as medication. They divided 123 people with depression into two groups. One group continued with medication; the other group had MBCT (mindfulness-based cognitive therapy) and could choose to continue with medication or not. Over 8 weeks, the MBCT group met and carried out group exercises, such as focusing on the present not the past. About 47% of the MBCT group had a relapse over the 15 months after the trial had ended, while those who continued antidepressant treatment without MBCT had a 60% relapse rate. It was thought that MBCT had given skills for life that drug treatment (e.g. Prozac) had not.

Evaluation of drug treatment

Strengths
- Drug treatments can work quite quickly, which gives a respite while a different or complementary treatment is considered. For example, depression can be treated with antidepressants for short-term relief, which can enable people to get to grips with other treatments, such as counselling, because they feel calmer.
- Drugs can be prescribed quite quickly and long consultations that might be needed for some forms of counselling or cognitive–behavioural therapy are avoided. To this extent the treatment can be seen as cheap, although drugs themselves can be costly.
- Atypical antidepressants have fewer side-effects so as research progresses, medication might be a better option.

Weaknesses
- It is possible that the use of drugs masks the problem but does not treat it. One symptom can simply replace another.

- Kane et al. (1988) found that between 10% and 20% of people do not improve if given drug therapy (although this presumably means that the others do improve in some way).
- Drugs may treat the symptoms, but it is doubtful if they address the cause of the disorder. Often the patient has to continue using the drugs, despite problems of dependency, tolerance and toxicity.
- Withdrawal symptoms can occur if drugs are discontinued, and there is often a relapse too. Hogarty (1984) claimed that 40% of patients relapsed within 6 months and 70% within 1 year. This means that drug treatment has to continue, which can be difficult if there is, for example, tolerance. Tolerance means that more and more of the drug is needed to achieve the same effect. Addiction can also occur.
- Side-effects can be a problem. Drugs often act by mimicking or blocking neurotransmitter movements in some way. A neurotransmitter is likely to have many roles in the nervous system. The drug might help with some of the symptoms of the illness, but may also affect other functions of the nervous system. Antidepressants, for example, can lead to sleepiness, dry mouth, nausea and sexual problems.
- A government study (2006) found that less than 50% of those on antidepressants become symptom-free and many relapse into depression again even if they keep taking the medication.

Evaluation points were also given for the use of drug treatment in schizophrenia. You can use some similar points when discussing drug treatment for depression. However, if using an example, remember to focus on the 'right' mental disorder.

Cognitive–behaviour therapy for depression

Beck (1967) emphasises how problems can develop when people distort their experiences. Someone who is depressed is likely to see only the bad things that happen. Cognitive therapy asks people to think again about their experiences and focus less on bad ones — or see them as less bad.

Beck used a behavioural approach too, in suggesting that one way to prevent negative thinking is to do something active, such as going for a walk. By doing active things there is the possibility of positive reinforcement when things go well (e.g. if people enjoy the walk or parts of it) and this helps with positive thinking.

The cognitive model identifies some unhelpful ways of thinking, such as catastrophising ('it will be a disaster'), overgeneralising ('I will never get this right') and 'should' statements ('I ought to be better than this'). Therapy can address these to help people rebalance their thinking so that it is more helpful ('sometimes I make mistakes').

A CBT session usually lasts about 50 minutes. The counsellor first sets up an agenda in collaboration with the client and they agree what the session will focus on. The core conditions (genuineness, empathy, unconditional positive regard and congruence) are maintained — this is taken from Rogers's client-centred therapy. Then tools are used to uncover, for example, negative automatic thoughts ('nobody likes me'), rules and assumptions ('if I always help everyone then they will like me'), and core beliefs ('I am unlovable') that can come from early experiences or some other trigger.

An example of a tool is the downward arrow technique where negative automatic thoughts can be examined to find a rule. For example, if a person thinks 'I am a bad mother', she can ask herself what that means to her. What does it mean to others if she is a bad mother (if that were true)? What does it mean about her that she is a bad mother (if that were true)?

CBT is just as suitable for anxiety, low self-esteem and other disorders as it is for depression; however, it has been used extensively for depression.

Evidence for the effectiveness of CBT

Stiles et al. (2006) looked at CBT and other therapies (person-centred and psychodynamic) over a 3-year period in 58 NHS settings in the UK. They found that no therapy stood out as being more successful than any other and all groups (some had art therapy, some had integrative therapy — there were various combinations) showed a marked improvement. So CBT itself was not shown as any more effective than other psychotherapies (an overarching term), but was effective.

> **Tip**
>
> When considering the effectiveness of CBT you can use the study mentioned earlier (p. 53) that showed that CBT compares well against medication (Kuyken et al. 2008).

Evaluation of CBT as a therapy for depression

Strengths:

- The individual is helped to recognise any problems and is taught to overcome difficulties, so it is likely that any solutions will be more lasting than with a therapy such as token economy, which is outside the individual's own control.
- Cognitive restructuring has been used successfully, for example, in stress management. By having a sense of control, a person is better able to cope with stressful situations.
- Studies have also found that cognitive therapy works for depression (e.g. Seligman et al. 1988). CBT is called 'evidence-based' because there is evidence for its effectiveness (e.g. Kuyken et al. 2008).

Weaknesses

- The therapies rely on rational individuals who can control their thought patterns, at least to an extent, so may only be suitable for certain individuals. Young children or people with psychoses may not respond to cognitive therapies. However, CBT has been used with schizophrenia, for example, particularly with regard to improving life skills.
- Evaluations have supported the usefulness of cognitive therapies for depression, but there are other studies that suggest either that a mix of therapies (e.g. cognitive therapy and drug therapy) would be more successful or that other therapies such

as social skills training might be more useful. Haaga and Davison (1989) found that it was important that the treatment matched the individual — someone with irrational thinking benefits from cognitive therapy, but someone with a social skills deficit benefits from social skills training.

- It may be that negative thinking comes from the depression rather than causing it. Some have reported that when the depression goes so do the negative thoughts; however, this just shows that the relationship is hard to demonstrate.
- Stiles et al. (2006) found that different psychotherapies were equally successful rather than CBT standing out — though the government has invested in Improving Access to Psychological Therapies (IAPT), and focused on offering CBT because it is evidence-based.

Treatments from other approaches

You need to be able to describe and evaluate one treatment or therapy from each of the five AS approaches; your course suggests two possibilities for each approach. In this whole section on clinical psychology, drug treatment (both for schizophrenia and depression) has been covered (from the biological approach), as have CBT from the cognitive approach and a community therapy from the social approach. Therefore, this section covers one therapy from the learning approach and one from the psychodynamic approach.

If you have covered a different therapy for any of the approaches, you might prefer to revise that instead of learning more.

A therapy from the psychodynamic approach: dream analysis

Freud developed the idea that dreams were the 'royal road to the unconscious' and could help to find out what was repressed in the unconscious. If repressed thoughts are released into the conscious, in theory they should no longer be troubling — so analysing dreams is one way of uncovering problem issues that are using energy and holding someone back.

The content of the dream symbolises unconscious thoughts. Freud thought that dreams were a means of 'wish fulfilment' allowing wishes in the unconscious to be fulfilled and, therefore, released.

Dream work involves the therapist in knowing a great deal about the individual so as to be able to suggest what the manifest content of the dream (what the dream is about according to the dreamer — what they remember of the dream) symbolises. The manifest content hides the latent (hidden) content, which is the wishes that are being repressed.

Evaluation of dream analysis as a therapy

Strengths
- Fonagy (1981) suggests that Freud's ideas question the appropriateness of a scientific rational approach to understanding people, so the common criticism that Freud's work is not scientific is not helpful because he could not measure his concepts scientifically.
- Freud's ideas about psychoanalysis (including dream analysis) have led to many different psychotherapies, such as client-centred therapy, humanistic therapies and CBT. These therapies have also drawn from other approaches, but it is widely thought that Freud's ideas about the role of mental processing in disorders helped to generate psychotherapies.

Weaknesses
- Shapiro et al. (1991) suggest that psychodynamic therapies are only sometimes successful with depression, perhaps because depressed people find it hard to engage with the process. Furthermore, the therapy takes time and requires intensive sessions, and so is expensive.
- Freud used case studies such as that of 'Little Hans', and these looked at unique individuals so it is hard to generalise the idea of 'dream analysis' to everyone.
- Masson (1989) discussed ethical issues and power issues between the analyst and analysand (client) — it could be claimed that Freud's therapy is unethical because it is not collaborative, for example, unlike CBT.

A therapy from the learning approach: token economy
Token economy programmes (TEPs) are based on operant conditioning principles, which suggest that a rewarded behaviour will be repeated. TEPs are a form of behaviour modification because they aim to change behaviour to desired behaviour.

Positive reinforcement involves giving a reward to someone for desired behaviour, for example to someone with schizophrenia who shows required social skills. Shaping is sometimes used, when what is desired is unlikely to be shown immediately — in this case the behaviour has to be shaped gradually and rewarded step by step as the behaviour gets closer to what is required.

Negative reinforcement is when a person wants to remove something unpleasant so they behave in such a way as to remove that negative issue. For example, if someone has a panic attack when out shopping, they may stop shopping to remove the threat of the attack. Negative reinforcement is not likely to be used so much in TEPs because that would mean threatening a person with something unpleasant which they then have to act to avoid.

Punishment is rarely used because it demonstrates what is not required but does not show what is required, and also tends to model aggressive or negative behaviour. However, sometimes it is used: for example, if someone with schizophrenia in a hostel breaks the rules often, they might not be allowed on a specific outing.

TEPs run along the lines of a planned programme of reinforcements where tokens are given for required behaviour, which can be exchanged for something desired (like watching a television programme or having a treat in the way of food). Tokens are given because this is manageable for staff; they are exchanged for desired rewards (this is the economy part); and there is a plan for how to achieve what is desired, so it is a programme.

Recall what you learned about operant conditioning in the AS approach.

Evaluation of TEPs

Strengths

- A Swedish programme was carried out in 2008 with 12 long-term schizophrenic patients. It was found that the patients' activity levels changed over the time of the programme towards what was thought to be desirable. Activities for two of the patients included stopping lip-biting, making more appropriate eye contact and stopping aggressive acts. Then the treatment was stopped and the activities returned to their original levels. When the TEP was reintroduced, the levels went back to desirable ones again. This suggests that TEP works (though perhaps there is a problem with maintaining any progress once the treatment stops). Five of the 12 patients were discharged during the 8 months of the programme and none of these five were readmitted during the 1-year follow-up.
- McGonagle and Sultana (2008) compared the use of TEP with standard care for those with schizophrenia. They looked at many studies. One of the studies suggested TEP was more successful than standard care and found that negative symptoms of schizophrenia had showed improvement after 3 months. The researchers concluded that, although there might be some effect on negative symptoms, more evidence was needed.
- The programme rests on well-researched theory (operant conditioning), and studies (such as animal studies) have shown that positive reinforcement works to change behaviour.

Weaknesses

- There needs to be a clear system of rewards so that everyone in the team understands how the programme works and acts on the same principles. This requires a lot of commitment from staff as well as training, which can be costly.
- There is a power issue in that the staff are given a lot of power over the patient which can be seen as undesirable and an ethical issue.
- There might be a problem in transferring the behaviour to outside an institution where the rewards are not present.

Studies in detail

For this part of the unit you need to know Rosenhan (1973), which is explained below. You also need to know one study that looks at schizophrenia: Goldstein (1988) has been explained in detail earlier (pp. 25–27), so is not included here. You also need to know a study in detail for your other chosen disorder, which here is unipolar depression. Here Brown et al. (1986) is explained.

You might prefer to use the study you learned in your course if it was not Goldstein (1988) or Brown et al. (1986); or you could use Gottesman and Shields (1966) as the study into schizophrenia (pp. 22–24).

Rosenhan (1973): 'On being sane in insane places'

Aims
Rosenhan 'sent' people to mental hospitals pretending to hear voices. They were diagnosed as having schizophrenia in remission (except one). His interest was in whether they would be diagnosed (they were), and how they would be treated when in the hospital (they made notes and observations). This was a study about abnormality and diagnosis, which investigated whether eight sane people who gained admission into different hospitals would be 'found out' (identified as sane). He wanted to see what it was like to be seen as 'insane'.

Procedure
Eight pseudo-patients (they were pretending) were involved; one was Rosenhan, and others were mainly professionals. Only the chief psychologist and hospital administrator where Rosenhan carried out the research knew about it; nobody else did. There were 12 hospitals used, in five different US states, and they were varied in character.

The pseudo-patients called the hospital for an appointment and arrived saying they had been hearing voices (which said words such as 'empty' or 'hollow'). Apart from that and changing some details so they were not recognisable, the participants gave accurate answers to any questions.

When they were admitted (all were) they behaved 'normally' in every way and, though they were given medication, they did not take it. All wanted to be discharged so they behaved very well and followed all instructions from staff.

In a second part of the study, staff at a teaching hospital were told that in the next 3 months one or more pseudo-patients would attempt to be admitted. Each staff member was asked to rate patients on a scale of 1 to 10 to indicate the likelihood of them being a pseudo-patient.

Results

The results discussed are for the first part of the study except where otherwise stated. The pseudo-patients were never detected. All but one were diagnosed as having schizophrenia in remission. 'In remission' meant 'able to be discharged'. There was nothing in the hospital records on the pseudo-patients that showed there had been any doubt about the diagnoses. The pseudo-patients spent an average of 19 days in the hospital, with a range of 7–52 days. Visitors and other patients felt the pseudo-patients were sane; during the first three hospitalisations, 35 out of the 118 patients on the admissions ward voiced their suspicions.

The normal family background of a pseudo-patient was interpreted as abnormal — for example, changing patterns of closeness between a 'patient' and his parents were seen as 'a long history of considerable ambivalence in close relationships' (p. 244). Three 'patients' had their writing diagnosed as part of their pathological behaviour — 'patient engages in writing behaviour' was recorded.

In the second part of the study, where staff were looking for pseudo-patients, 41 patients were judged by at least one staff member as being a pseudo-patient, although (as far as Rosenhan knew) there were no pseudo-patients.

Conclusions

Rosenhan stated (p. 242) that 'any diagnostic process that lends itself so readily to massive errors of this sort cannot be very reliable'. He also concluded that, once diagnosed as having a mental disorder, someone is seen in that way and their behaviour judged accordingly.

Use the Rosenhan (1973) study when discussing the DSM and the validity and reliability of diagnosis (pp. 33–36).

Evaluation of Rosenhan (1973)

Strengths

- The kinds of hospital were varied so generalisation was possible, and 12 hospitals were involved, again strengthening the findings and allowing generalisation.
- There was validity in that the pseudo-patients behaved as themselves except for the 'voices', which they only mentioned on admission. This validity could be seen in that other patients and visitors questioned their diagnosis.
- Using 8 people in 12 hospitals meant the study was replicated and, as the same results were found, this gives the study reliability.

Weaknesses

- The study rested on lies — the pseudo-patients did say they were hearing voices and in the second part of the study staff were told that there would be pseudo-patients. So perhaps it is not surprising that the pseudo-patients were labelled as schizophrenic or that the staff in the second study 'found' some pseudo-patients. The validity is compromised.

- In the decades since the study was carried out practices have been changed and also there is now care in the community, so the findings may not now apply. It might be wrong to conclude that mental illness is still hard to diagnose.

Brown et al. (1986): a study on depression

Aims
- to see whether crisis support protects against the onset of depression even if there is low self-esteem and lack of general support
- to see if lack of support and low self-esteem are vulnerability factors in depression
- to see if support from a husband, partner or close relationship reduces the risk of depression (the study involved only women)

Procedure
Women with husbands in a manual occupation, with at least one child under 18, and aged between 18 and 50, were recruited through their GP; 435 women were chosen who fitted the requirements, and 395 were involved in the first part of the study.

At first contact, measures of self-esteem and personal ties were taken for the women, and psychiatric histories were collected. Twelve months later they were checked for any onset of psychiatric disorder over that period, and measures of social support and life event stress were also taken.

Interviews were used to gather the data, carried out by experienced interviewers. Some women were interviewed intensively to check for reliability. There was inter-rater reliability.

Results
- In all, 353 women agreed to a follow-up interview (89% of the original sample).
- There were 50 cases of depression at first contact and those women were excluded.
- Therefore 303 were interviewed to see if they had developed depression over the 12 months. About half of them (150) had had a severe event or major difficulty and 32 women had the onset of depression.
- Of those 32 women, 91% had experienced a severe life event in the 6 months before the onset of depression (involving loss, failure or disappointment).
- If self-esteem was looked at as well as a provoking agent (severe life event), 33% who had a negative evaluation of self developed depression in response to a provoking agent compared with 13% who developed depression in response to a provoking agent, but who did not have a negative evaluation of self.
- This suggests that those with low self-esteem are more likely to develop depression when faced with a provoking agent than those with high self-esteem.
- With regard to social support, 92% of those women who had core crisis support said it was helpful. Of those women who felt let down with regard to support, 42% (14 of 33) developed depression. Of those without support either at first contact or later, 44% (4 out of 9) developed depression. It seems that social support is an important factor in whether someone develops depression or not.

Conclusions

- Those who were married or had a close tie were less likely to develop depression (unless they confided in their husband and then felt let down).
- Low self-esteem is implicated in the onset of depression after a provoking agent. Self-esteem might in itself be linked to whether a person has social support.
- A provoking agent seems to be necessary for the onset of depression in most cases.

Evaluation of Brown et al. (1986)

Strengths

- The interviews gave the required depth and detail for analysis of complex issues.
- There was inter-rater reliability, which strengthens the findings.
- Interviewing tends to gather valid data given the depth and detail, and trained interviewers using semi-structured interviews should be able to explore in the necessary depth.

Weaknesses

- Qualitative data were 'reduced' to quantitative data to give percentages, which means some of the information could have been lost — such as the role of the husband.
- This was a study of working-class women with one child under 18 at home and in a specific age range, so generalising to all women might not be appropriate.

Evidence in practice: key issue and practical

You will have carried out a practical based on a key issue from the application. You will need to be able to describe the key issue and also answer questions based on your practical, which was designing a leaflet. For example, understanding unipolar depression could be taken as the key issue, and the practical could involve producing a leaflet about it to help someone just diagnosed with this condition.

Issues and debates

This section looks at issues and debates but there is only a limited amount of information here because you will have already covered most of what you need to know. This part of the unit requires you to draw on your learning from the previous three units and clinical psychology.

Introduction to issues and debates

For this part of the unit you need to cover the following areas:
- definitions of terms
- contributions to society from the approaches (AS) and applications (A2) — two for each approach and one for each of the three applications you studied
- ethical guidelines and principles for research, both when working with human participants and when using animals, and two studies that involve ethical issues
- research methods — three types of experiment, observation, questionnaire, interview, content analysis, correlation and case study — and one study for each; planning and evaluation of a study of your own
- key issues from the approaches (one for each) and for each of the three applications you studied (one for each)
- four debates — ethnocentrism and cultural issues, psychology as a science, the extent to which psychology is about social control, and the nature–nurture debate
- the application of knowledge of psychology to new situations

This material is briefly reviewed in the following sections under seven headings: definitions, contributions, ethics, methods, key issues, debates, and new situations. In each case material is suggested rather than explained so you will need to use your textbooks and other resources to check your understanding. Where possible, suggested material is found elsewhere in this guide and the page number given.

Definitions

You need to be able to define the following terms, all of which are dealt with in later sections:
- content analysis (p. 74)
- ethnocentrism (p. 79)
- social control (p. 83)
- token economy (p. 57)
- practitioner (p. 84)
- science (p. 81)
- nature (p. 86)
- nurture (p. 86)

Contributions

You need to be able to describe and evaluate:
- two contributions for each of the five AS approaches

- one contribution for each A2 application that you have studied (i.e. one contribution each for two applications from criminological, child, health and sport psychology, as well as one contribution from clinical psychology)

In some cases one contribution can cover more than one purpose: for example, drug therapy is a contribution from clinical psychology and also from the biological approach. The brief list that follows should help your learning.

Tips

- Use the material you already know (such as drug therapy or token economy) but make sure you discuss it in terms of contributions to society. This means describing and evaluating as usual, but also finishing by saying how the treatment (or idea or whatever you are discussing) has helped society (or not); for example, by helping to make the course of a mental disorder less severe for an individual in society.

- You may have studied contributions other than the ones given here for a particular approach or application — often there are many you could choose — so you might prefer to revise those. Notice as well the link between a contribution to society and a key issue for society. Many contributions can be presented as key issues but make sure the way you word your answer suits the question.

The social approach

- The social approach has contributed to our understanding of prejudice by using social identity theory — so recall that theory and make sure you learn its strengths and weaknesses as a contribution to society.
- The social approach has also contributed to society by offering an explanation for blind obedience. It can help to show why soldiers under orders can do what are seen as atrocious things, as in Abu Ghraib Prison.

The cognitive approach

- The cognitive approach has contributed by helping society to understand problems with eyewitness testimony and how it might not be reliable.
- It has also contributed by developing the cognitive interview as a way of improving the accuracy of testimony.

The psychodynamic approach

- Society has benefited from the use of psychoanalysis as a therapy, not only in itself but also because it seems to have generated other similar psychotherapies. (In your study of clinical psychology, you may have looked at dream analysis as a therapy from the psychodynamic approach (pp. 56–57) — it is used within psychoanalysis so you can use your learning about that here.)
- Society has benefited from the explanation of dreaming as well, if only to see that thoughts can be hidden in symbols and that dreams might represent some underlying wish that is not being fulfilled. There are other explanations for

dreaming, such as the biological one, activation synthesis, and it is useful to be able to see dreams from another, less scientific point of view, to focus on the individual rather than what people have in common.

The biological approach

- Society has benefited from the study of sex assignment, which has shed light on why some people feel they are wrongly sexed and need treatment to help them to become 'themselves'.
- Explaining autism using biological concepts has been a great contribution to society as children with autism (and families of children with autism) have benefited from greater understanding of their needs and abilities.

The learning approach

- The learning approach has contributed to society by offering systematic desensitisation as a treatment for phobias, anxiety and related disorders.
- The learning approach has helped society in the treatment of mental disorders by explaining how token economy can help to obtain desired behaviour and to eliminate undesired behaviour. (Within clinical psychology you may have studied token economy as a therapy developed within the learning approach (pp. 57–58) so use your learning to explain this as a contribution to society.)

Criminological psychology

Criminological psychology has contributed by helping society to understand problems with eyewitness testimony and how it might not be reliable. (The study of the reliability of eyewitness testimony is part of the criminological application as well as falling within cognitive psychology, so that contribution can be used here as well.)

Child psychology

In explaining autism using biological concepts, child psychology has made a great contribution to society, as children with autism (and families of children with autism) have benefited from greater understanding of their needs and abilities. (Biological explanations for autism fall within child psychology as well as the biological approach, so that contribution can be used here too.)

Health psychology

The suggested contribution here is the use of drug therapy for substance misuse. Drug therapies work in similar ways and affect synaptic transmission, so when considering drug treatments, whether for mental disorder or substance misuse, very similar issues apply, which is why this contribution is suggested here. You can use some of the information found within the clinical psychology section (pp. 46–47 and pp. 53–54). However, you will also need to know about specific drug treatments, such as replacement heroin for heroin addiction.

Sport psychology

A contribution that sport psychology has made to society is in understanding good coaching practices, such as the use of imagery and goal-setting techniques.

Clinical psychology

You will have covered many contributions to society within clinical psychology because the treatments will be useful for society, given that there is evidence that they are effective. Drug therapy has been discussed in this guide as a treatment for both schizophrenia (pp. 45–46) and depression (pp. 52–54), so that seems a good suggestion as a contribution to society.

Ethics

For this section you need to know five ethical guidelines for using human participants in psychological studies and five ethical principles when using animals in psychological studies. You also need to be able to describe and evaluate two studies with regard to ethical considerations.

Guidelines for using human participants

You will have studied the British Psychological Society guidelines of competence, deception, informed consent, right to withdraw and debrief, both in the social approach for Unit 1 and the learning approach for Unit 2. It makes sense to choose those five ethical principles and to review them here. It would be useful to know each guideline, be able to define it, have an example of its use and be able to evaluate its usefulness, for example by using a study to show where the guideline was recognised or not used and why.

Summary of five ethical guidelines for using humans in psychological research

Ethical guideline	Description	Evaluation/comment
Competence	Having the qualifications and ability to carry out the study safely and ethically or asking someone else about it.	Ethical committees now would check that someone is competent to carry out the study, so this guideline should be adhered to. Milgram showed competence by researching beforehand what others thought would happen.
Consent	Participants have to agree to take part and should be informed as far as possible so that consent is informed. Children and others tend to be special cases.	Often consent is not informed consent because telling a participant all about the study means the results will not be useful. If Milgram said the shocks were not real, for example, participants would not be obeying in a real sense.

Debrief	After the study a debrief is carried out to explain everything, and this can cover the problem with obtaining uninformed consent. The debrief should include explanation of the findings.	A debrief is difficult in a naturalistic observation if people are in a public place and not told about the study. They may not be contactable. Otherwise, however, debriefing should not be difficult. Milgram gave a thorough debrief to participants in his studies.
Deceit	Deceit is related to uninformed consent because often a study requires deception. Uninvolved people can be asked if they would mind being involved and from their responses the agreement of uninformed participants could be assumed (presumptive consent) — there are ways to ensure ethical practice even if there is deceit.	A debrief helps with deceit because participants can be informed about what has happened and if they do not agree to their results being used, they can withdraw them. Prior consent (participants agree in general to take part without detail) or presumptive consent can contribute to ethical practice. Milgram deceived his participants in more than one way.
Right to withdraw	Participants should have the right to withdraw from a study at any time and must be told about it and reminded. They must also be able to withdraw their results at the end of the study.	It is not usually hard to give the right to withdraw, although naturalistic observations (where participants do not know they are being observed) do not allow it. Right to withdraw the results is given in the debrief and, except for observations, is usually possible.

Principles for using animal participants

You will have studied ethical principles for using animals in research when you looked at the biological approach for Unit 2, so revise your learning. You need to know five principles; suggested ones are summarised in the table below. Again you need to be able to explain the principle, give an example, and then evaluate in terms of problems in applying the ethical principle or how it clashes with practical needs.

Summary of five ethical principles for using animals in psychological research

Ethical principle	Description
Care over caging and social environment	Any caging and/or social environment must be suitable for the species.
Avoiding discomfort and stress	Any stress and/or discomfort must be kept to a minimum.
Rules about the use of anaesthetics	Anaesthetics must be used appropriately by someone who knows about them.
Number of animals used	No more animals must be used than necessary.
Look for alternatives	Alternatives to using animals must always be sought, such as using humans or computers.

A useful evaluation point would be to consider who decides what is ethical with regard to animals, as we as humans are making the rules. If, for example, we think that our species is the most important, then we would be less worried about behaving in an ethical way with regard to animals. However, if we felt that as animals ourselves, we ought to treat other animals in the same way as humans, then we would want ethical principles for animals to be very similar to those for humans. Take care, in fact, not to use ethical guidelines for humans when talking about animals. In some ways it is true that animals cannot give consent or ask to withdraw, but currently these are not issues we consider with regard to animals (you could comment on this in evaluation).

It is often hard to separate practical and ethical issues in the use of animals, so take care to talk about ethics if the question specifies ethical issues.

Describing and evaluating ethical issues

The information about the five ethical guidelines with regard to humans and five ethical principles with regard to animals should be enough for a question about describing and evaluating ethical issues in psychological research. If you have prepared definitions, examples and evaluation points then that should suffice. You need to know in detail two studies where ethical issues arise (see below) and you can use these also in a question about ethical issues in general.

Two studies and their ethical considerations

You need to prepare in detail two studies and their ethical considerations so choose two that you know well and consider their ethics. You will almost certainly remember Milgram's (1963) study, which is a useful one when discussing ethics in research with humans. Other suitable studies include Hofling et al. (1966), Watson and Rayner's (1920) study of Little Albert (if you covered it), studies into daycare such as Melhuish et al. (1990) and many others. All psychological research is likely to involve ethical issues, though perhaps studies on memory and forgetting are less easy to discuss in ethical terms. As studies need to be suggested for the method section that follows, comments about their suitability for use in a question about ethics are made there.

Methods

For methods, you need to:
- know nine research methods in reasonable depth, with both description points and evaluation points, and with one study for each method
- be able to plan and evaluate a study of your own

• be able to evaluate psychological studies that are given to you with respect to the research methods used

These areas are discussed in the sections that follow.

Nine research methods and studies using them

The nine methods are as follows: three types of experiments (laboratory, field and natural experiments), observations, questionnaires, interviews, content analyses, correlations and case studies. You need to be able to describe each method (for up to 6 marks perhaps) and evaluate it. You need to revise one study for each method and be ready to describe and evaluate it in detail. Studies are suggested below for each of the nine methods. In summary, you have to be able to:
• describe the method
• evaluate the method
• describe the study in detail
• evaluate the study in detail

Method 1: Laboratory experiments
• Craik and Tulving (1975) used the laboratory experiment to look at levels of processing (Unit 1).
• So did Bandura et al. (1966) when they looked at how children might copy aggressive behaviour (Unit 2).
• If you have looked at criminological psychology, you will have covered Loftus and Palmer's (1974) study, which used the laboratory experiment method to test whether changing the verb in a question led to different judgements of the speed of a filmed car. If you are using eyewitness testimony as a contribution (or key issue) then it might be useful to choose Loftus and Palmer (1974) here.

Revise one of these studies in detail — or choose one of your own. Recall that you studied laboratory experiments in the cognitive approach for Unit 1.

Method 2: Field experiments
• Hofling et al. (1966) did a field experiment to look at obedience in a natural setting, and you probably covered that study, which is also useful for ethics, so perhaps worth choosing here. You can also use Hofling et al. (1966) if discussing obedience as a contribution to society of the social approach.
• If you studied criminological psychology you may have looked at Yarmey (2004), which is also a field experiment, this time looking at eyewitnesses and recall in the natural setting. If you are using eyewitness testimony as a contribution (or key issue), then it might be useful to choose Yarmey (2004) here.
• Godden and Baddeley (1975) is a field experiment that you might remember from Unit 1 — they looked at how context affects recall.

You studied field experiments in the cognitive approach for Unit 1.

Method 3: Natural experiments

You studied natural experiments in the cognitive approach for Unit 1. However, you may not have covered a study using this method in your course — unless perhaps you studied Charlton et al. (2000) when looking at criminological psychology. As a natural experiment has not been explained elsewhere, Charlton et al. (2000) is covered in some detail here. There are other natural experiments but they are not easy to find, as the independent variable has to be naturally occurring, which happens rarely.

Charlton et al. (2000)

Aims

- to see the effect of television on children's behaviour when it is introduced
- to use the opportunity of finding a society without television but about to introduce it, so that its impact could be judged and studied

Procedure

Researchers went to a remote island called St Helena to look at the behaviour of the children by recording their playground behaviour on video. Then their behaviour was recorded again after the introduction of television. This was to look at both prosocial and antisocial behaviour to see if either had changed after the introduction of television.

The data were gathered by observation and video recordings; however, this study tends to be seen as a naturalistic experiment because the independent variable (television or not) was naturally occurring. Because there was a clear IV and DV this can be seen as an experiment; also, the researchers were looking for cause-and-effect conclusions.

Results

- They found little difference in prosocial behaviour after the introduction of television.
- They found little difference in antisocial behaviour after the introduction of television.
- There were 9 changes out of 64 comparisons that were made.

Conclusions

- It was thought that watching television did not lead to changes in behaviour such as more or less aggression, which did not match what laboratory experiments like Bandura et al. (1966) had found.
- It was thought that perhaps this community had strong social and community ties and support, which was why television did not seem to have much impact on the children's behaviour.

Evaluation

Strengths

- This study was ethical as television was being introduced in any case — the researchers did not manipulate the independent variable, so did not interfere much with the situation. They did introduce video recording but this avoided the impact of observers.

- Before and after measures were clear — observations before television was introduced were carried out in the same way as observations afterwards — so cause-and-effect conclusions could be drawn.

Weaknesses
- It is possible that being part of a study affected the behaviour of the children, who were well-behaved when being recorded.
- The study took place over 5 years and other changes over that time may have affected the findings. Television may have led to more or less aggression but other changes, perhaps cultural ones, may have counteracted the effect.

Method 4: Observations

You studied observations in the learning approach for Unit 2. In the main, observations in psychology are naturalistic ones, taking place in the natural surroundings of the participants. However, Ainsworth developed the strange situation procedure, which entailed a structured observation. It is suggested here that you use naturalistic observations and not the strange situation procedure, so that there is no doubt that you are discussing the observational method.

You may have covered Parten (1932) if you studied child psychology and you may have looked at observations in your study of daycare. The Robertsons used observation when studying children in hospitals and devising their theory of attachment and detachment. However, you may not have covered a study using observation if you did not look at child psychology, so one is given in some detail here. Observation is in fact quite a common method in psychology but does not appear very often in the material for your course.

Melhuish et al. (1990)

The observation was part of a longitudinal study that also used interviews and questionnaires. The observational part is explained here; it was done to gather direct qualitative data to support the other data gathered.

Aim
- to see how four different types of care for young children during the day affected their behaviour

Procedure

There were four groups of children that made up the independent variable. Three groups had parents who were both earners and so used daycare. The other group belonged to families which had a single earner and a non-working mother and which did not use daycare. This last group was the 'home group'. The three groups other than the home group were either day nursery children, those with a childminder or those cared for by other relatives.

So there was the home group, day nursery group, childminder group and relatives group. The question was whether the different daycare arrangements affected the child.

There were 255 London families contacted by phone. Background information was gathered by questionnaire. The children were visited at 5 months, 11 months, 18 months and 36 months of age. A total of 246 children took part in the 18-months visit where interview data, questionnaire data and observational data were gathered.

Children were observed in their daycare or home setting using two 1-hour observations. For various reasons some of the families were not included and in the end, the study involved 44 children in the home group, 34 in the day nursery group, 59 in the childminder group and 19 in the relatives group.

Observations took place during free play and involved recording the child's activity every 10 seconds. Behaviour was not included if it did not have 70% inter-observer reliability or more. Overall there was 86% inter-observer agreement with regard to adult interactions (which were also recorded) and 82% agreement with regard to children's activities. Two observations were made on different days to check for stability of behaviours.

Results
- With regard to responsiveness, it was found that the home and relatives groups were more responsive than the nursery group. The home group was also more responsive than the childminder group.
- With regard to affection and emotional behaviours, the nursery group showed fewer affection responses than the other groups.
- Aggression was greater in nurseries, but low overall.
- With regard to language use by the child, the nursery group showed the least use of language compared with the other three groups. The childminder group showed lower language use than the home group as well.

Conclusions
- Overall it was thought that the four types of daycare had different outcomes for the child with regard to specific behaviours.
- Individual play, crying and gestures did not differ between the groups but responsiveness, aggression, language use by the child and affection were areas of behaviour that did seem to show differences between the groups.
- Attention, joint play and group activity showed differences too.

Evaluation

Strengths
- There is inter-observer reliability in the findings that were reported, so the study is shown to be reliable.
- The children were observed during free play when they could choose their own activities, which should have led to fair comparisons between the four groups.

Weaknesses
- The nurseries were privately owned and not well resourced. If different nurseries had been used there might have been different results.
- Only 18-month-old children were observed so perhaps the findings should only be generalised to that age group.

Method 5: Questionnaires
- If you studied sport psychology you will have covered the Boyd and Munroe (2003) study that used questionnaires to compare the use of imagery in climbers and in track and field athletes.
- Craft et al. (2003), another study from the sport psychology application, also used questionnaire data in that they did a meta-analysis of studies which had all used the same questionnaire.
- If you studied health psychology you may have looked at Ennett et al. (1994), a study that looked for a link between smoking and friendship groups and used a questionnaire to gather the data.

You studied questionnaires in the social approach for Unit 1. In case you have not covered a study using questionnaires, Boyd and Munroe (2003) is given in some detail here.

Boyd and Munroe (2003)

Aims
- to look at how climbers and track and field athletes use imagery
- to see if they use imagery differently because there are different needs for the two sports
- to see if beginner and advanced climbers use imagery differently

Procedure
The study used 38 track and field athletes and 48 climbers, some of whom were beginners.

There were two questionnaires used, the SIQ (sport imagery questionnaire) for the track and field athletes and the CIQ (climbing imagery questionnaire) for the climbers. The CIQ was a version of the SIQ amended to make it relevant to climbers, for example by replacing references to 'competing' with 'climbing'.

Each questionnaire had 30 items each asking for a 7-point rating of how often the respondent used imagery in those particular circumstances, where 7 was 'very often' and 1 was 'rarely'.

Results
- There was a high response rate, with track and field athletes being different from climbers in how they used imagery.
- They were also different in the type of imagery they used. for example, planning a climb used different imagery from imagining winning a track event.

- Not much difference was found in the use of imagery between beginner and advanced climbers.

Conclusions

- It was concluded that people participating in different sports do use different types of imagery depending on what the imagery is being used for.
- Some imagery is to motivate success and some is to plan how to achieve something, for example.

Evaluation

Strengths

- The study used the SIQ, which has been used in other situations and studies, so findings can be compared.
- The study could easily be replicated because the questionnaires were fixed and the statements all rated by all participants.

Weaknesses

- The CIQ was different from the SIQ in that the CIQ did not refer to competition — perhaps the different wording affected the replies.
- There did not seem to be a great deal of difference between beginner and advanced climbers and they rated their ability themselves. If their experience levels were not very different, perhaps that is why there was little difference found in their use of imagery.
- Self-report data tend to be unreliable — perhaps because they depend on how the respondent feels at the time, which may be affected, for example, by recent experiences of performing well or badly in their sport.

Method 6: Interviews

You studied interviews in the social approach for Unit 1. In clinical psychology two studies used interviews to gather data. Goldstein (1988) used interviews to find out if women had a different experience of schizophrenia from men (pp. 25–27), and Brown et al. (1986) to see how social factors affected whether women developed depression or not (pp. 61–62). As both these studies have been covered in detail earlier in this study guide, it is suggested that you use one of them as an example of interviewing. In fact Gottesman and Shields (1966) also used interviewing within their study (pp. 22–24) so you could use that as well — but focus on the interviewing, not the collection of data by other means.

Method 7: Content analyses

You will have done a content analysis as part of your study of the applications for Unit 3, so review your own practical and how content analysis is undertaken.

However, you may not have studied a content analysis that someone else has done, so an example is covered in some detail here. A **content analysis** (a key term) is a method in which primary data are gathered from sources that already exist, such as media sources (journals, newspapers, television programmes and so on). The idea is to search the content for themes and tally how often those themes appear.

Cumberbatch and Gauntlett (2005)

Aims
- to find out how much smoking, alcohol and drug abuse feature in television programmes watched by 10–15 year-olds
- to find out how they are treated on television

Procedure
The researchers focused on the ten programmes most watched by 10–15 year-olds, which included 70% soaps. The study was carried out from August to October 2004 and 256 programmes were involved in the analysis, all broadcast before the 9.00 p.m. watershed.

Categories that were tallied involved scenes where alcohol, smoking or legal or illegal drugs featured. There were 2099 scenes analysed. Material that was counted included observed or implied alcohol, smoking or drug-related behaviour and references to alcohol, smoking or drugs. Visual representations were also counted, such as a drink in a scene.

Results
- Alcohol featured more than smoking or drugs in the most popular television programmes. Alcohol-related scenes occurred about 12 times each hour, smoking-related scenes about 3.4 times each hour, and drug-related scenes about 1.7 times each hour.
- Only 4% of the programmes had no occurrences of the target scenes.
- Both drinkers and smokers had large roles in scenes — 37% of the major characters were drinkers and 4% were smokers.
- Messages about alcohol were more or less neutral in 84% of the scenes and 91% of the smoking messages were neutral; 57% of the drug references carried an anti-drug message and 40% were neutral

Conclusions
- Alcohol features quite a lot, smoking less so and drugs even less.
- Alcohol and smoking are mostly referred to in a neutral way, rather than in a positive way promoting their use. Most drug references were either negative or neutral.
- Quite a few of the major characters tend to be drinkers, while far fewer are smokers.

Evaluation

Strengths
- There are no ethical issues with a content analysis, which only involves counting instances of categories in existing material (though perhaps results and conclusions can have an impact that might have ethical implications).
- There is generallsability with regard to the findings, at least to programmes watched by 10–15 year-olds, as many different programmes were chosen.

- It was checked that the programmes used were the top ten that the age group watched, which was a valid measure.

Weaknesses
- Of the programmes, 70% or more were soap operas and all showed before the 9.00 p.m. watershed, so perhaps findings should only be generalised to those programmes.
- The study was about modelling and how children might pick up on television portrayal of alcohol, smoking and drugs. However, children also have models in their families and elsewhere. A content analysis does not show a causal link.

Method 8: The correlational technique
You studied correlations within the psychodynamic approach for Unit 2. A correlation is not really a research method as such, because correlational data can be collected by different methods such as questionnaires and interviews.

If you studied criminological psychology you might have covered Madon et al. (2003), who used correlational analysis to see if mothers' expectations of their child's alcohol use were self-fulfilling.

You might not have looked at a study that used correlational analysis so, as Craft et al. (2003) has already been mentioned as using questionnaire data, and they analysed the data using correlational analysis, that study is given in some detail here.

Craft et al. (2003)

Aims
- to see how two different types of anxiety (somatic or physical anxiety, and cognitive anxiety) relate to one another and to self-confidence
- to see how somatic anxiety, cognitive anxiety and self-confidence relate to sporting performance

Procedure
The researchers brought together the findings of different studies which had used the same questionnaire to look at anxiety and self-confidence — this was a meta-analysis. The data had been gathered in the same way so they could be compared.

The data from 29 studies were analysed to see how far cognitive anxiety, somatic anxiety and self-confidence were related both to each other and to sporting performance. Participants had rated themselves for both types of anxiety and for self-confidence so the scores were self-report data.

Results
- In general, it was self-confidence that related to sporting performance rather than anxiety.
- Cognitive anxiety related to somatic anxiety. The result of the correlational analysis was r = 0.52 (quite a high positive correlation) — as cognitive anxiety rises so does somatic anxiety.

- Cognitive anxiety related to self-confidence and the result was r = −0.47 (quite a high negative correlation) — as self-confidence rises cognitive anxiety falls.
- Somatic anxiety related to self-confidence and the result was r = −0.54 (again quite a high negative correlation) — as self-confidence rises somatic anxiety falls.

Conclusions

- Both types of anxiety seem to be related to self-confidence — the more confident a performer the less anxious they are, which makes sense.
- As the two types of anxiety are closely related as well, and both have a similar negative correlation with self-confidence, it seems possible that somatic and cognitive anxiety are not in fact separate.

Evaluation

Strengths

- They drew on 29 studies so had large amounts of data from the same questionnaire, which is a strength of a meta-analysis.
- The data were collected using the same questionnaire, which had been standardised, so the data should be reliable.

Weaknesses

- Perhaps it was not valid to separate cognitive and somatic anxiety — they seemed to rise together and also they were both similarly related to self-confidence, as if they were the same thing. Alternatively, perhaps they could not be separated by using a questionnaire.
- The data were collected for different purposes and as they are other researchers' data, they might not be validly compared.

Method 9: Case studies

- You will have studied the case study of Little Hans so you could use that here.
- If you have looked at child psychology, you will know about the case study of Genie and the case study of the Czech twins.
- Within the psychodynamic approach you may have studied Dibs, another case study child.
- Money (1975) studied a pair of twins, looking at gender development — this is a case study you covered in the biological approach.

You studied case studies within the psychodynamic approach for Unit 2.

Planning a study

Note that you may be asked to plan your own study from a scenario that is new to you. You could be asked to give aim, hypotheses, design, procedure, ethical considerations and how results could be analysed (including choice of statistical test). You are also likely to be asked to evaluate your study in some way. You might not need to give all this information, but be ready to.

Draw on all your knowledge and understanding of methodology — including the studies given above and their strengths and weaknesses — when designing your own study. You could practise this part of the course. Choose an area you are interested in (perhaps men and depression) and plan an appropriate study (using questionnaires, interviews or perhaps PET scanning). You could repeat this exercise as often as you like to gain confidence in your understanding of methodology.

Evaluating psychological studies

You might be asked to evaluate a study that is given to you. Draw on your ability to evaluate all the studies you have covered throughout your course — there are a great many of them — and think about evaluation issues such as GRAVE (generalisability, reliability, application, validity, ethics).

You may not have considered making suggestions for improvements to a study. Choose two studies that you know really well — such as Godden and Baddeley (1975) or Hofling et al. (1966) — and note down a few ideas about how each one could be improved. If you are stuck, think about using a different methodology, improving it with regard to ethical issues, or trying it in another culture.

Key issues

You need to review eight key issues: one for each of the five AS approaches and the three applications you covered (two applications for Unit 3 and clinical psychology as the third application). You will have chosen a key issue for each of these or you could prepare another one. Suggestions for each of the approaches and applications are given here to help (see the table below).

Where suitable, the contribution to society is also suggested as the key issue to help you limit the material you have to prepare, but be sure to focus precisely on any question. If it is about a contribution, then present your answer in that way and explain why it contributes. If about a key issue, say why it is such an issue for society. A key issue is any issue of relevance to today's society.

Be ready to describe the key issue and then explain it using concepts, theories and research from the approach or application as appropriate. You will need the same material if you use the same issue as a contribution to society.

You are asked to use your knowledge of the approaches and applications, as well as research methods and ethical issues, when commenting on the key issues. Using concepts, studies and theories from the approach or application will cover using knowledge of the approaches and applications, but remember to bring in ethical issues and methodological issues where appropriate (such as where laboratory evidence is used to show the unreliability of eyewitness testimony and you can, therefore, criticise the validity of the evidence).

Suggested key issues related to the AS approaches and A2 applications

Approach or application	Suggested key issue
Social approach	How to reduce prejudice, or explaining blind obedience to authority such as at Abu Ghraib Prison
Cognitive approach	The unreliability of eyewitness memory, or how successful the cognitive interview technique is
Psychodynamic approach	When and if psychoanalysis is successful as a therapy, or whether dreams have meaning
Biological approach	Understanding and helping regarding sex assignment (and mis-assignment), or helping to explain autism
Learning approach	The effectiveness of systematic desensitisation to cure phobias, or the effectiveness of token economy programmes to achieve more adaptive behaviour
Criminological psychology	The unreliability of eyewitness memory
Child psychology	The effects of daycare on a child's development
Health psychology	The effectiveness of drug therapy with regard to drug addiction
Sport psychology	How to be a good coach to help with sporting success
Clinical psychology	The effectiveness of token economy programmes

Debates

There are four debates you need to cover: psychology and cultural differences, psychology and science, psychology and social control, and the nature–nurture debate. Some of this material you will have looked at but there may be other material you have to learn. The focus here is on the material you may not have covered. All of the terms that you need to define are found in this section, except content analysis, which was defined earlier.

Psychology and cultural differences

You need to be able to describe and evaluate issues of ethnocentrism and also look at cultural bias when carrying out cross-cultural studies.

Ethnocentrism
Ethnocentrism (a key term) refers to being focused on one's own culture and is a type of bias. If a researcher interprets study findings gathered in a different culture using their own cultural views, it is likely that they will be ethnocentric — focused on their own culture — and, therefore, biased in their interpretation of the findings.

Bartlett (1932) showed, using studies like the War of the Ghosts, that we reconstruct our memories from schemata and so memories are not like a tape recording of facts.

So it makes sense to think that researchers are ethnocentric in their views — they see the world through their own frames of reference.

It is useful to know about bias such as ethnocentrism so that researchers can try to avoid it; for example, by using ethnography, a method that immerses the researcher in the culture they are studying so they are less likely to have ethnocentric views. Malinowski is a well-known anthropologist and ethnographer who studied peoples in the Trobriand Islands and immersed himself in their culture so he would avoid ethnocentrism. A problem, however, is that even if the researcher gathers in-depth data from the other culture and learns the language and customs, misunderstandings are likely to arise in both linguistic and non-verbal areas.

Clinicians also have to watch for ethnocentrism, for example when diagnosing someone from the DSM, as discussed earlier in the material on clinical psychology (pp. 36–38).

Cross-cultural research

If you studied child psychology you will have covered the work of Ainsworth, whose strange situation procedure has been used in many other cultures to see if her three attachment types were still found. It is unclear whether the strange situation is transferable or not, as studies tend to find different proportions of the different types of attachment and this might be because the procedure is not understood in the same way in different cultures. For example, in Germany independence is valued more, so more independent babies might be expected. The findings might be affected by culture. However, in practice the majority of the studies find that the most common type of attachment is securely attached, which does suggest that attachment types are universal and that the procedure is transferable.

Fouts (2008) looked at a father's role among two peoples in Africa, both foragers. A father's involvement was not the same in both societies. In some societies gender roles are more flexible than in others. This suggests that there are cultural differences between most societies — something to keep in mind when drawing conclusions from studies.

One issue is that cross-cultural research is the only way of comparing different cultures to look for universal laws of behaviour. If something (like an attachment pattern) is found in all cultures then it seems that it might be universal and come from human nature. If, however, something differs between cultures then it is likely to come from nurture and environment.

The strange situation has been used universally. However, one criticism is that researchers have assumed that secure attachments are best, but this may be an area where cultures differ — it might be that secure attachments are seen as 'right' in some countries while in other countries a different kind of attachment might be preferred (e.g. mothers might protect their children less to encourage independence). If that is so, then other types of attachment might be more common in some countries, not because of insensitive mothering but because of cultural differences.

> **Tip**
>
> Although there could be any question about the debates, it would be useful to pre-
> pare an essay looking at cultural differences in psychology so you can make sure you
> have enough material. However, always answer the actual question given, and do not
> give a prepared essay such as 'describe and evaluate cultural differences in psychol-
> ogy' unless that is the actual question asked. Use the material to answer the question.

Psychology and science

You need to be able to discuss the issue of whether psychology is a science, and 'discuss' tends to mean 'describe and evaluate'. You have already covered a lot of methodological issues, all of which can be used to discuss whether psychology is a science. However, a few more issues are presented here to add to your knowledge and understanding.

The hypothetico-deductive model

Karl Popper uses the hypothetico-deductive model to define what is meant by '**science**' (a key term). He suggests that knowledge builds on existing theories. A researcher looks at a theory and from it generates a hypothesis — this is deduced from the theory. Then the hypothesis is tested inductively, which means gathering data through our senses (empirical data). So for Popper, science means using the hypothetico-deductive model — a theory, a hypothesis, testing, and then accepting or rejecting the theory accordingly.

For example, a researcher might start with the levels of processing theory, and generate the hypothesis that someone who wrote a shopping list out and added imagery would remember more items from the list than someone who just wrote the words out. (For example, one list might be just 'butter, bread, sugar, tomatoes and juice' while the other might be 'butter on the bed, bread on the stairs, sugar in the hall, tomatoes on the television and juice in the sitting-room chair'.) To test this hypothesis, an independent groups design could be used where one group has the pure list and the other uses imagery in some way. Then if the people in the group who used imagery (and so added meaning) remember more items than those in the other group, the theory would be confirmed — semantic processing is best.

Psychology uses the hypothetico-deductive model a great deal, but it does not always do so. Case studies do not really have hypotheses, but have aims and gather in-depth detailed data about individuals to meet those aims. Little Hans, for example, was studied using a case study method, rather than an experimental method with careful controls like the one described above (for testing whether semantic processing is best). So in general, case studies are not doing science in Popper's sense.

Reductionism versus holism

Another way of looking at sciences is that they reduce things into parts to study them more effectively. Biology, for example, might study genes, hormones or neurotransmitters to see how the brain works or to see how gender develops. This is a reductionist approach because it looks at parts, which is very valuable for the

purpose of gathering scientific data that has been carefully tested so the theory can be built up.

However, reductionism has been said to mean that the 'whole' is ignored. Someone who thinks they were wrongly sex-assigned at birth is a 'whole' person and giving them different hormones, for example, to make changes might not be appropriate on its own. The opposite of reductionism is holism — looking at the whole person rather than parts of the person. So psychology that takes a reductionist approach is likely to be more scientific than psychology that takes a holistic approach.

In your course most of what you have studied takes a reductionist approach, though the Little Hans study is more holistic, as is the case study of Genie. Brown et al. (1986) (pp. 61–62) look at a range of social factors that affect whether women develop depression rather than just a few factors, so in that sense they take a broader view. On the other hand, they do present data as quantitative, by looking at the factors separately, which is reductionist.

The subject matter of science

Psychology might be said to be more scientific if it is about 'scientific' subject matter such as genes, hormones, neurotransmitters, specific behaviours or how sense data enters the brain. In your course you have studied a lot of science — the research methods, the biological, cognitive and learning approaches, as well a lot of clinical psychology and health psychology (e.g. drug treatments). However, there has been subject matter that is less scientific, such as dream analysis (pp. 56–57) and how prejudice is formed.

Elements of study that make something scientific

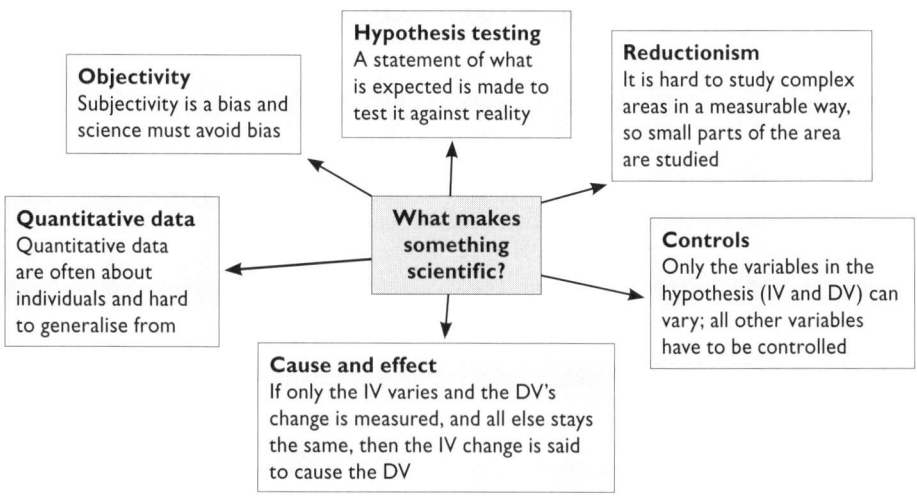

The five approaches

You need to be able to discuss the five AS approaches in terms of how scientific they are in their methods and content. The table below provides a summary.

The five AS approaches and how far they might be seen as scientific

Approach	Scientific	Not scientific
Social	Experiments, objectivity, cause-and-effect conclusions	Ethnography, qualitative data, focus on the individual
Cognitive	Experiments, objectivity, scientific subject matter (brain and processing)	Processing hard to measure, some qualitative data (e.g. case studies)
Psychodynamic	Aimed at general (universal) laws	Concepts not measurable, case study method, qualitative data, focus on individual functioning, subjectivity possible (interpretation needed)
Biological	Subject matter (e.g. genes, hormones), experiments, objectivity, universal laws	Twin studies, case studies, subject matter can be hard to measure
Learning	Experiments, cause-and-effect conclusions, objectivity, measurable	Social learning theory includes cognition such as motivation and attention

Tip

Look at the five approaches and your three chosen applications and make a list of what in them is scientific in its subject matter or methodology and what is not. Then you can use these examples in this section.

Psychology and social control

For this section you need to know about issues of social control in various areas of psychology, including drug therapy, token economy, classical conditioning and the influence of the practitioner in treatment and therapy. You have to cover ethical and practical implications of social control.

Social control (a key term) refers to how psychology can be used to control members of society, often for the good of other members of society, or for other reasons. Social norms and customs keep people under control to an extent. Consider the definition of abnormality as that which goes against social norms (pp. 29–30), which shows how much society needs people to abide by social norms (otherwise they are 'treated' in some way).

Ethical issues with regard to social control

Ethical issues concerning social control involve questions such as:
- Who should have control over others?
- When is control appropriate?
- Who should be controlled?
- What means are appropriate?

Consider these questions when answering any question which asks about social control or examples of how psychology can be involved in social control.

Practical issues with regard to social control

Practical issues with social control involve questions such as:

- How should or could someone control someone else?
- What practical implications are there to social control (such as taking care of members of society who are seen as needing to be controlled)?

Drug treatment is a way of controlling people, as are token economy and classical conditioning. **Practitioners** (a key term) are those providing the therapy, such as those working for the health service, and therapists. They have power over patients and clients and this, too, is an important issue of social control. In dream analysis the analyst has the power, which is a standard criticism of psychoanalysis (see Masson 1989 and pp. 56–57). In the token economy programme (TEP) those administering the programme and giving out the tokens are in control, which is seen as a criticism of TEP (pp. 57–58).

Drug therapy

Drug therapy is discussed in the clinical psychology section in relation to both schizophrenia (pp. 45–47) and depression (pp. 53–54). You need to be able to describe drug therapy and evaluate it, particularly with regard to ethical and practical issues. Drug therapy is also used for substance misuse, and you could use that material here if you covered that application.

Token economy programmes

Token economy programmes (a key term) are explained in the clinical psychology section as a therapy from the learning approach (pp. 57–58). You may also have come across them in one of your other applications as they are used, for example, to treat aggression, as covered in the criminological application. Use what you have learned about token economy, as well as what you know about operant conditioning principles, to explain how such programmes can be a form of social control. Be ready to discuss ethical issues concerning such control and practical issues too (such as training needed for staff). Include problems with the power of the practitioners. Evaluation points about token economy will include practical and ethical issues (p. 58).

Classical conditioning

Classical conditioning is a form of social control both when used as a treatment and when used in other areas such as advertising. You could look at one or both of these areas — and there are others.

Advertising

In advertising, a product is often linked to an unconditioned stimulus to generate, eventually, a conditioned response. For example, for a man the sight of a beautiful woman can be arousing, so having a beautiful woman in a car advertisement can link the car to the arousal. As this is done without the individual realising, it is a form of social control. There might be little harm in doing this in television advertisements but the principle can be used for more sinister purposes by those controlling the media in a country. This is about power and ethics.

Systematic desensitisation

In clinical psychology, classical conditioning principles are used in treatment such as systematic desensitisation. You may have looked at this therapy when you were studying the learning approach for AS. It is used to help someone with an association they want to get rid of, and works by replacing that association with a more helpful one.

For example, a phobia of flying can be treated using systematic desensitisation. First, the patient or client must learn to relax, by practising deep muscle relaxation, as that will be the response that replaces the fear. Then the concept of 'flying' is gradually introduced — perhaps using a picture of a plane first, then a film, then a simulation, then having the person sit in a real plane on the runway — until finally reaching the goal, which is to take off. At each of these stages the person relaxes until they feel able to move on to the next phase, so that systematically they are desensitised to flying. They replace the fear response with the relaxation response.

In the flying example, the desensitisation is helpful for the person and is their choice — but the method could be used as social control if it was thought to be desirable for someone to replace one association with another. The therapist, as in all therapies, has the power, which can be misused (though this is not to say therapists do misuse their power).

Aversion therapy

Another treatment that uses classical conditioning principles is aversion therapy. For example, someone who is an alcoholic and wants to stop drinking alcohol can pair alcohol with something unpleasant to stop them drinking it. First, an emetic drug is introduced that would make someone sick — or instead use can be made of a drug that the person *believes* will make them ill (because they have been told so). Then that drug is paired with the alcohol and the person is made either to feel sick or to believe they will be sick. They should then learn that alcohol makes them feel sick or pair the alcohol with the threat of feeling sick, and so stop drinking.

This might be helpful but the therapy could perhaps be used without the person's permission — that would be unethical and would involve issues about the use of power. For example, in the past homosexual men have been given such 'treatment' (pairing a shock with a picture of a nude male, for example) to 'cure' them. Of course, homosexuality is no longer considered to be a mental health disorder and is not in the DSM (though it was previously), but this is an example of how classical conditioning can be used as a form of social control and how ethical and power issues are involved.

Power of the practitioner

The power of the practitioner has been explained above when looking at how drug therapy, token economy and classical conditioning can be used as forms of social control. Even cognitive–behavioural therapy (pp. 54–56), which is a collaborative approach and where great steps are taken to avoid the situation where the therapist has power over the client, is caught up in the problem of the client (and others) perceiving that the therapist has power.

The nature–nurture debate

Nature (a key term) is what humans are born with, their genetic characteristics and their biology. **Nurture** (a key term) refers to environmental influences and experiences that affect how someone develops. It could be said that some characteristics come from our nature and some from our nurture, although it is generally accepted that, in fact, the two interact all the time and development is affected by both our nature and our nurture — this is the interactionist approach. However, much research is done to distinguish what in our development and characteristics comes from our nature and what comes from nurture — and this is the nature–nurture debate.

Twin studies

One way to study what is nature and what is nurture is to use twin studies. If MZ (identical) twins share a characteristic more than do DZ (non-identical) twins, then it is thought that at least some of that characteristic comes from nature. Twin studies are explained in the clinical psychology section (pp. 21–24), and an example of a twin study given there (Gottesman and Shields 1966) shows how the method has been used to provide evidence for a strong genetic influence in schizophrenia.

Cross-cultural studies

Cross-cultural studies can also show what laws of behaviour are universal, which suggests they are part of human nature. For example, studies using the strange situation procedure, carried out in different cultures, strongly suggest that there are three forms of attachment and that secure attachments are the most frequent in all cultures. So forming a secure attachment could be part of our nature. This is discussed in child psychology and you may have covered it there. Cross-cultural studies are briefly explained earlier in this Issues and Debates section too (pp. 79–81).

Approaches, applications and examples of the nature–nurture debate

During your course you will have come across various instances where the nature–nurture debate is discussed. The table below gives some examples for you to recall and revise.

How approaches and applications link to the nature–nurture debate

Approach/ application	Nature	Nurture
Social	Perhaps that people have evolved to act as agents in society	Focuses on how society affects people, including interactions of in-groups
Cognitive	Information processing in the brain takes place in a certain way and brain structures serve different functions with regard to thinking	Cues in the environment are used to help us to remember; how we encode something from the environment can affect forgetting/ recall
Psychodynamic	People have the id, ego and superego and are guided by unconscious forces	Parents and society give the superego and conscience and so we learn to fit with society

Approach/ application	Nature	Nurture
Biological	Hormones, neurotransmitters, brain structures link with the genetic blueprint, as do maturational processes	The environment from conception onwards affects maturation and development
Learning	Reflexes are innate, as is the tendency to learn by association and reward (how we learn)	What we learn comes from the environment, including all our experiences
Criminological	Can include whether someone is born criminal, perhaps linked to aggression and brain structures (or hormones)	Includes the effect of the environment on becoming criminal, such as the self-fulfilling prophecy
Child	Babies are born with a tendency to form attachments and to develop language, among other features	Environment, such as privation and deprivation, affects development
Health	Drugs affect neuronal transmission at the synapse, for example	Treatments for drug addiction seem to have to include removing environmental cues that might lead to relapse
Sport	Aspects of personality such as introversion or extroversion can come from biological make-up; the level of arousal can affect performance	Arousal can come from environment; other issues such as need for achievement can be learned (or innate?)
Clinical	Mental disorders can come from nature such as schizophrenia and depression, where there might be an element of inherited tendency	Mental health issues seem to be affected by the environment — for example, those with social support seem to be less affected by depression

New situations

In this Issues and Debates section you can also be asked to apply what you have learned to new situations. It is hard to give examples of this — you need to tackle what comes up using what you know. However, there are some general areas in psychology that are often useful for explanations and these are listed below as a guide. Use this list as a checklist for what you could include if you are stuck in a question that is asking you to apply your understanding to a situation you have not thought about before. Some general points of guidance are also included after the list.

Some useful explanations

- Much of human behaviour can be explained using **social learning theory**. Look for what behaviour could have been imitated and suggest that the behaviour

referred to in the question has come from modelling, which involves the principles of social learning. This is about nurture.

- The **psychodynamic approach** is often useful as well. Consider how the behaviour being referred to could be driven by unconscious wishes and desires, possibly stemming from early experiences. You can use your imagination to some extent here, because you might not have information about early experiences. You could make plausible suggestions, for example that a child has desires that are repressed, such as needing more closeness with their parents. This can involve nature and nurture.

- **Operant conditioning** principles are useful, because a lot of behaviour can be explained by showing how it has been rewarded (or not) and so is displayed (or not). This is about nurture.

- **Biological explanations** are almost always possible. You can refer to genes and suggest that any behaviour that is mentioned in the source (the new situation) comes from genetic tendencies in some way. Alternatively, you could refer to neurotransmitter functioning — could the behaviour be explained by brain processing? Hormones are also useful to explain some behaviours. Usually, though, it is the genetic explanation that is easier to identify. This is about nature.

General points

- Use **studies** as evidence for your points from theory. For example, when talking about social learning theory bring in Bandura. When talking about the psychodynamic approach bring in Little Hans and Freud. When talking about genes, bring in Gottesman and Shields to show the influence of genes.

- Use **methods** to evaluate studies and theory. For example, if giving a psychodynamic explanation you could mention that a lot of evidence comes from case studies, whose findings were not easily generalisable, and some of which were not very reliable.

- If you can, comment on **nature–nurture** issues (e.g. on how far a behaviour might come from nature, and that environment is also likely to have an effect). This is a useful evaluation point.

- If you can, comment on whether, or to what extent, an explanation is **scientific**, as that too is an evaluation point.

Questions
&
Answers

This part of the guide presents questions in two sections, one for each part of Unit 4: Clinical Psychology, and Issues and Debates.

The questions for **Clinical Psychology** are divided into five subsections:
- Definition of the application
- Methodology and how science works
- Content
- Studies in detail
- Evidence in practice: key issue and practical

The questions for **Issues and Debates** are divided into six subsections:
- Definitions
- Contributions
- Ethics
- Methods
- Key issues
- Debates

It is helpful to work on one area at a time for your revision and exam practice. Choose one area that you have studied within Clinical Psychology or Issues and Debates and revise the material using this unit guide. Work through the questions for your chosen area, answering them yourself without reading the advice on how to answer the question and without reading the answers given. Then mark your own answers, and read through the advice on what is required. Did you interpret the question successfully? Read through the answers given and note where the marks are awarded. Finally, read through the examiner's comments to see what full answers should include.

Note that Issues and Debates is a section of the specification that covers your past learning, so questions here can be wide-ranging and you will need to be ready to use your knowledge and understanding in different ways. The questions in this guide are just a small sample of the kinds of things you can be asked about. Write some questions of your own (e.g. 'describe...', 'evaluate...', 'explain...', 'compare...') to practise. The questions chosen here are often stretching ones — as it is less helpful to give more 'standard' ones that stick to 'describe' and 'evaluate'. This does not mean that you should expect all the questions to be 'stretching'.

Examiner's comments

All questions and answers are followed by examiner's comments. These are preceded by the icon *e*. They indicate where credit is due and point out areas for improvement, specific problems and common errors such as poor time management, lack of clarity, weak or non-existent development, irrelevance, misinterpretation of the question and mistaken meanings of terms.

Clinical psychology

Question 1

Definition of the application

(a) Define what is meant by primary and secondary data. (4 marks)

(b) What is the difference between reliability and validity? (2 marks)

(a) There are 2 marks for each type of data, so you could explain each and give an example of each to get the full marks.

(b) There are 2 marks for the difference. You could briefly define each and then add a sentence summarising the difference.

■ ■ ■

Answers

(a) Primary data are data that are gathered first-hand by the researcher(s) using their own methods and controls. ✓ For example, Gottesman and Shields (1966) interviewed their participants to look for symptoms of schizophrenia or related psychosis and interviews gather primary data. ✓ Secondary data are data that are second-hand and taken from another source or someone else's data. ✓ For example, Gottesman and Shields (1966) used hospital records to identify twins where at least one had a diagnosis of schizophrenia so they used someone else's data, which was secondary data for Gottesman and Shields. ✓

This answer is thorough and clearly earns all 4 marks. It shows the benefit of giving examples to show understanding.

(b) Reliability refers to consistency — if you do a study again and get the same results, the results are said to be reliable. Validity refers to measuring what you say you are measuring, such as measuring eyewitness memory when you do a laboratory study where students watch a film and answer questions. ✓ This example might not show validity as the students are not eyewitnesses as such. The difference is that a study can be done over and over again so be reliable but may lack validity. Loftus and Palmer's laboratory study of eyewitness memory is a good example of the difference — the findings are consistent (reliable) but might not be about real life (valid). ✓

This is a very clear answer and worth more than 2 marks really, but there are only 2 available. It is hard to answer this question without this sort of detail. You are likely to get one mark for knowing what the two terms mean, and the second mark for giving a difference.

Question 2
Methodology and how science works

(a) Identify two research methods that have been used to study schizophrenia. (2 marks)

(b) Explain one way in which the issue of validity arises in clinical psychology. (3 marks)

(a) Here you just need to list two research methods that have been used in the study of schizophrenia. In practice probably most methods have been used in that way but it is better to stick to the ones you have studied to avoid giving one that has not been used (perhaps symbol analysis?).

(b) Think about the validity of diagnosis and explain what is meant by it, and that should give you the 3 marks.

■ ■ ■

Answers

(a) Twin studies ✓ and animal experiments. ✓

This clearly gets the two marks.

(b) Validity of diagnosis is an important issue in clinical psychology. If someone with a mental disorder is wrongly diagnosed, as happens with manic depression, which is hard to diagnose because it has symptoms in common with other mental disorders, then they are likely to receive the wrong treatment and not to be helped. ✓ Validity is when a diagnosis is right, in that it explains the symptoms appropriately and suggests appropriate treatment. ✓

There are 2 marks here rather than 3. Validity is explained briefly and then an example is given. More could be said: for example that lithium is a suitable treatment for manic depression while antipsychotic drugs may not be, so the wrong treatment will affect the individual.

■ ■ ■

Question 3
Content

(a) Describe the DSM approach to classifying mental disorders. (4 marks)

(b) Explain how issues of validity affect diagnosis. (4 marks)

(c) Compare and contrast *two* definitions of abnormality. (12 marks)

(d) Outline *one* possible cause of one of the mental disorders you have studied. (3 marks)

(e) Evaluate the possible cause of the disorder you described in question (d). (6 marks)

(f) Outline *one* treatment that is used for a mental disorder that you have studied. (3 marks)

(g) Evaluate the treatment you outlined in (f). (4 marks)

(a) There are different versions of DSM; you should describe DSM-IV-TR as it is the most recent (at present — another one is due very soon). You can gain 1 mark for each point made and further marks for any points that are developed. A list of the five axes is likely to gain you a maximum of 2 marks if the list is not expanded upon. It is useful to be able to describe DSM, so it is worth preparing this question even though it may not be in the specification.

(b) One mark is likely to be available for saying what validity is in this context — don't just say what validity is in a methodological sense. You need to give evidence to show whether diagnoses have been valid or not. Make sure you say enough for 4 marks.

(c) In this essay question you need to describe briefly two definitions of abnormality and then make points about where they are similar and where they are different. You could evaluate them both and show in that way how they are similar and different, as strengths and weaknesses can be compared.

(d) Note that 'one' is emphasised. You need to focus on one possible cause only, and not give an outline of more than one. If you do give more than one, they will all be marked and the one gaining most marks will gain credit. The reason the question asks for 'possible cause' rather than 'cause' is that very little in psychology is proved and mental disorders are not yet fully understood. The question is just asking you to write about one of the 'causes' you studied. Always read the question carefully to make sure that you answer it correctly.

(e) You must refer to the same 'possible cause' (for the same disorder) you discussed in question (d). You need to make evaluative points. You could give six separate points, or fewer than six points, with some clearly elaborated. One way of evaluating a factor is to contrast it with another (for example, saying the social cause you chose does not take into account biological causes). However, note that only 1 mark is likely to be awarded for giving an alternative — no further marks would be awarded for describing that cause as you should be focusing on the one you are evaluating.

(f) Here there are 3 marks for the outline of one treatment. Use one of the treatments for schizophrenia that you studied or one treatment for your other

chosen disorder. In the answer here, phobias is chosen as the disorder, although depression is the second disorder discussed in the Content Guidance section of this guide. Phobias are chosen to show you that other disorders are of course acceptable choices (there is a list in the specification — stick to the one you studied in class).

(g) There are 4 marks for evaluating the treatment you outlined in (f) above. Make sure you stick to the same treatment, and if giving examples to illustrate a point, make sure they apply to the disorder you are using.

■ ■ ■

Answers

(a) DSM-IV classifies mental disorders using symptoms and characteristics. It has five axes to create a full picture of the patient. ✓ The axes are: clinical disorders, personality disorders and mental retardation, general medical conditions, psychosocial and environmental problems, and the global assessment of functioning. ✓ The last one has a scale that takes into account how the person is functioning, for example in work and social relationships. The scale goes up to 100, with 100 being very good functioning. ✓ The psychiatrist takes all the axes into account rather than diagnosing from just one of them. ✓ The DSM is used widely across different countries and care is taken to take cultural issues into account.

> This answer earns all 4 marks. Saying that there are five axes gains 1 mark and saying what these are gains a further mark (as it is a list it might get 2 marks but don't take that chance). Then the last axis is expanded upon to get another mark. The comment that more than one aspect is taken into account when diagnosing earns the final mark, and adding a bit extra about its use across different countries is wise, as it helps to make sure of the 4 marks. It is useful to add more even when you think you have written enough.

(b) For a diagnosis to be valid, it must measure what it is supposed to measure. But a diagnosis will not be valid if it is not reliable. ✓ There are different types of validity here, such as eteological. The most interesting is predictive validity, which looks at the validity of choosing the correct treatment; this is essential. ✓

> This answer scores 2 marks out of 4. The first sentence is rather general and could refer to validity with regard to research methods, but the second sentence helps to clarify it a little. One mark is given for these two pieces of information, neither of which is very clear. Etiological validity is not explained (note the incorrect spelling), but predictive validity is outlined in more detail and a good point is made about the importance of getting the treatment right. Another mark is given here. The point needed to be expanded for a further mark to be earned. Another mark could have been achieved by providing an example of how the wrong diagnosis, leading to the wrong treatment, shows the importance of valid diagnoses.

(c) Two definitions of abnormality are deviation from a statistical norm and deviation from a social norm. Deviation from a statistical norm means that 'normal' is defined as being what most people do and say, and 'abnormal' refers to any behaviour that most people would not exhibit. The idea is that if there are sufficient people in a sample, most people lie within two standard deviations either side of a mean average — this is normal distribution. This would take care of about 96% of any population. Using the definition that abnormality is deviation from the statistical norm, then 2% either side of that 96% of the population is abnormal (by definition). If we say that in IQ the standard deviation is around 15, and the mean is 100, this means that 70 is the dividing line for the bottom 2% and 130 is the dividing line for the top 2%. So anyone with an IQ of below 70 or above 130 is defined as abnormal.

If the definition of abnormality is deviation from a social norm, then a different criterion is used, this time looking at what people normally do in a social sense. Unlike statistical norms, these norms are measured by what society approves of. Most people do socially acceptable things, and this is 'normal'. Once someone does something unacceptable, this is abnormal by this definition.

When comparing the two definitions, it can be seen that someone with a very high IQ is abnormal given the first definition, and indeed having a high IQ is not a social norm either, so the two definitions are similar. However, having a high IQ is not socially unacceptable, so is not abnormal using the second definition. In this way, the two definitions disagree. We are more likely to agree that people who are abnormal in the sense of mentally ill are likely to be doing things that are socially unacceptable (such as using disorganised speech in schizophrenia), whereas just being statistically abnormal does not mean someone is mentally ill. In fact, disorders such as depression could almost be said to be statistically quite common and not just found in a small percentage of the population.

This answer balances descriptions of the two definitions of abnormality with comments about their similarities and differences. This answer is marked using levels. The marker would look for evidence of both description and comparison for both definitions, in order to get beyond the halfway level of 6 marks. This answer does describe both definitions clearly with examples, so would reach top marks for that area of the answer. The answer is also clearly expressed, again reaching top marks for communication skills and use of terms. There is, however, not quite enough comparison. Comparison points are made, such as where the definitions are similar and where they differ, but more would be useful. It could perhaps be explained that the DSM takes into account both social norms (such as the level of general functioning) and statistical information (such as how long depressive symptoms have been experienced, and logging behaviour that is statistically infrequent such as hearing voices). A bit more depth would ensure full marks but this essay should just get into the top band.

(d) Schizophrenia is thought to be genetic. Studies of MZ twins, who share 100% of their genes, show that they are quite a lot more likely both to suffer from schizophrenia than DZ twins, who share 50% of their genes like any other pair of siblings. These studies come up with different concordance rates for MZ twins, but the rate tends to be around 50% (e.g. Gottesman and Shields 1966). ✓ Others have looked at brain structure and claimed that differences in structure, for example in size of ventricles, are connected with schizophrenia. ✓ The dopamine hypothesis suggests that schizophrenia is a result of excess dopamine, which is a neurotransmitter that is involved in the brain sending messages. ✓ It is possible that the differences in brain structure, such as size of ventricles and the problem with excess dopamine, both stem from genetic causes so this is taken as one possible cause — genes. ✓

> This is a thorough answer. There could have been a problem because it could be argued that there are three different biological causes in this answer — genes, brain structure (ventricles) and neurotransmitter functioning. It is because the answer has drawn these three together under a 'genes' heading that it is taken as discussing one possible cause. Notice how you can guide the examiner in this way and that you must justify that your 'possible cause' is 'one' and not many. You have probably studied one biological explanation — either genes or dopamine — so it would be better to stick to that and give more depth to get the 3 marks.

(e) However, although it seems that genes have a role in the development of schizophrenia, if only genes were responsible we would expect there to be a 100% concordance rate in MZ twins, and this is by no means the case. There could be a genetic predisposition for it. ✓ Also, not all those with schizophrenia have enlarged ventricles, and it is hard to see whether such brain differences cause the illness or are caused by it. ✓ As anti-schizophrenic drugs tend to work by blocking excess dopamine, this is evidence for the dopamine hypothesis. ✓ However, again it could be that the schizophrenia causes the excess dopamine and not the other way around, and it is also hard to show that the excess dopamine comes from genetic causes. ✓

> This answer is likely to get 4 of the 6 marks. It is quite detailed, dealing with each of the 'genetic' causes separately. The first marking point could be more fully explained by showing how there is nearer a 50% concordance rate for MZ twins, which suggests 50% is down to environment. The idea of a predisposition could be explained to be a mark on its own. Evidence from studies such as Gottesman and Shields (1966) would also gain marks, and other evidence as well would be useful if the genetic cause is the 'one' focused on. Similarly, for the dopamine hypothesis, evidence from studies is useful in evaluation. You could also get 1 mark for suggesting a non-genetic cause such as the 'environmental breeder' hypothesis as an alternative explanation.

(f) Flooding is a behavioural technique used to help overcome phobias. People are immersed in their fear and their anxiety levels then rise considerably. Anxiety levels can only rise to a certain extent before the energy needed to maintain them must run out, so the anxiety level should fall. ✓ As the exposure to the feared object continues, the individuals should feel less anxious, and then should interpret that as being cured of their phobia. ✓ The idea rests on principles of classical conditioning. The original situation is that the object gives a fear response and the final situation should be that the feared object gives a relaxed response. ✓

    🖉 There is enough detail here for the full 3 marks. A reader who did not know anything about flooding beforehand would learn what it was about. You might not know about flooding, so see whether you now understand the treatment (it is a bit like systematic desensitisation, p. 84).

(g) The main problem with flooding is that it is very unethical and involves a great deal of anxiety. ✓ It cannot be used to treat some disorders either, because it is based on classical conditioning principles, so it relates only to reflexive responses like fear. ✓

    🖉 There are two very good clear points here but they only get 2 marks so more is needed. You could mention that classical conditioning theory was developed using animal studies and findings from these (such as Pavlov's work) may not be generalisable to humans, so perhaps using such principles to treat humans is not appropriate. You could also give named evidence about the effectiveness of flooding.

■ ■ ■

Question 4
Studies in detail

    (a) Outline the procedure of two studies that you have looked at in detail within clinical psychology. One should be Rosenhan (1973). (6 marks)

    (b) Compare the procedures that you outlined in (a). (4 marks)

    (c) With regard to one study of schizophrenia, describe the findings. (4 marks)

    (d) Evaluate the study that you described the findings of in (c). (3 marks)

    🖉 **(a)** First give the procedure of Rosenhan (1973) for 3 marks and then give the procedure of one of the other studies you looked at in detail, either the one that looked at schizophrenia or the one that looked at your other chosen disorder. Make sure you identify the other study in your answer. Remember to

focus only on what was done — the procedure — not on the aims, results or conclusions.

(b) For the two procedures give points they have in common and points of difference, and try to give **4** different points (though there are other ways of getting the marks, such as elaboration). The two procedures have to be the ones you used for (a).

(c) Describe the results and/or conclusions of a study of schizophrenia and try to give 4 points (though you can gain marks by elaboration). You can describe just results or just conclusions or both (and/or).

(d) Evaluate the study of schizophrenia that you studied. Give strengths, weaknesses or both. Note that this has to be the same study you chose for (c).

███

Answers

(a) Rosenhan asked eight people (including himself) to go to a mental hospital and report hearing voices but otherwise to answer any questions 'normally'. ✓ Twelve different hospitals were used and the individuals went on their own to each one. ✓ When they were admitted they were to make notes and record how they felt being a patient in such a hospital. ✓

Brown et al. (1986) used interviewing to find out about social support. They used women who had working-class husbands and at least one child under 18, and they obtained their sample through the women's GP. ✓ They asked questions at time one, which was the start of the study, and found out about social support and friendships as well as about depression and life events. ✓ Then they interviewed the women again after 12 months to find out who had developed depression and whether factors like social support related to the onset of depression. So they asked the same questions again. ✓

> ✐ This answer gets all 6 marks and there is a lot of detail. The only point that is not well elaborated is the point about using 12 hospitals but this is additional information and is useful, so a mark was given.

(b) Rosenhan used a field study and the study was in a natural setting up to a point, though of course not the natural setting of the participants. It was the natural setting of the people being observed — the staff at the hospital. Brown et al.'s study was also in the field, in that the women were interviewed in their own setting, so it was a field study too. ✓ Rosenhan used eight people because in a way they each did case studies of their stay in the hospital, whereas Brown et al. used a great many women in their study so their study might be more generalisable. ✓ Then, again, Rosenhan used a range of people and genders, whereas Brown et al. used working-class women each with a child under 18, so perhaps generalising would be harder, even given the larger sample. ✓ Rosenhan carried out his study in five states in the USA and Brown et al. carried out their study in the UK. It is possible that social support factors differ between the UK and USA and that mental health institutions are different in the UK and USA (and other countries), so being in different countries might make a difference to their (separate) findings. ✓

There are four comparison points here and all are well elaborated. This answer shows how fully the point must be made to get the mark.

(c) Goldstein (1988) found that women do have an easier course through schizophrenia than men. ✓ They have fewer rehospitalisations and shorter lengths of stay. ✓ She found that what had happened before the onset of schizophrenia affected the rehospitalisations more than the length of a stay. ✓ Also social functioning affected lengths of stay more than the number of rehospitalisations. ✓ So perhaps women had more successful social functioning than men.

This is a thorough, detailed list of results of the study so all **4** marks are given.

(d) Goldstein (1988) used interviewing, which can be criticised because the data need interpreting so there might be subjectivity, ✓ but on the other hand, the strength is that data is detailed and in depth. As she wanted to know about issues such as premorbid functioning and social functioning (needing in-depth detail), interviewing was a successful strategy. ✓ She was able to count rehospitalisations and lengths of stay and so she had quantitative data, which are objective and, therefore, scientific. ✓

This earns all **3** marks. Some useful evaluation points are given, both strengths and weaknesses, and there is some discussion, rather than a list of points, which adds to the quality of the answer.

■ ■ ■

Question 5
Evidence in practice: key issue and practical

(a) Describe a key issue that you have studied within clinical psychology. (4 marks)

(b) You will have prepared a leaflet based on your key issue. Answer the following questions with reference to your leaflet preparation and the leaflet itself:

(i) Explain the audience that you prepared the leaflet for. (3 marks)

(ii) Give one design decision you made and explain with reference to the content of the leaflet why you made that decision. (3 marks)

(iii) Give another design decision that you made and explain it with reference to the audience you were preparing the leaflet for. (3 marks)

(a) This question is not asking about clinical psychology as such but about the key issue you looked at. You need to say what the issue is and why it is a key issue for society.

(b) (i) You need to outline the audience as well as explain why you chose that audience. For example, why do they need to know the information?

(b) (ii) Choose one of the decisions and explain it. An example might be omitting certain information as it might be unethical to include it and upsetting. You should focus more on the content being upsetting than the audience being upset, although you can talk about the audience as well.

(b) (iii) Choose a different design decision and then comment on why you made that decision with regard to the audience. You should focus on the audience and why they need that information, for example, or why you chose a format that would suit them.

■ ■ ■

Answers

(a) A key issue is what might help with depression. Depression is common in UK society and has consequences such as someone not being able to work or even go out. ✓ This costs society as well as being a great cost to the individual in terms of low mood, low self-esteem, sleeplessness (or oversleeping) and lack of motivation. ✓ Drug treatments can work after a few weeks (such as Prozac) but many do not want to take medication as there are side-effects. ✓ Psychotherapy can work but there are many different forms of psychotherapy and it is hard for people to get access to them, as well as hard to make an informed choice. ✓ Treating depression and reducing the onset of depression as well as reducing the course of the illness are important to society.

This answer is clear and gets all 4 marks. There is some content from clinical psychology here, such as the symptoms of depression and a mention of drug therapy. However, much of this is what someone with depression would know so is not theory as such and is necessary to explain the key issue.

(b) (i) I chose to prepare a leaflet on treatments for depression aimed at someone who has just been diagnosed with depression. ✓ They would need to know the choice of treatments, as a GP might prescribe medication without making another suggestion, or might make suggestions that the patient does not understand or know enough about at the time. ✓ A leaflet to take away would be helpful so that they can research the different treatments in their own time and make an informed choice. ✓

There are 3 marks here; the focus is clearly on the audience, which is what the question requires.

(b) (ii) In my leaflet I chose to include as many treatments as I could but to focus more on psychotherapies than on explaining the different medication. ✓ I did this because the medication sounds complex and in fact the GP is likely to decide what is suitable rather than the patient, whereas with regard to psychotherapies, the individual might have more choice and might like to know more about what is available. ✓ So I gave information about drug therapy but with less space allocated to it than to psychotherapies. I focused a lot on CBT because that is an evidence-based therapy and can be obtained free through the NHS, but I explained other forms of psychotherapy too. ✓

This answer is thorough and gets all 3 marks. The focus is clearly on the content of the leaflet (therapies for depression).

(b) (iii) In my leaflet I chose not to use the biological scientific terms for the drug treatments that I mentioned because I felt that the brand names were both more familiar and less threatening. So for ethical reasons, I was careful how I wrote about drug therapies. ✓ I was aware that the audience involves people who are depressed so the leaflet had to avoid anything threatening where possible. ✓ That is another reason for focusing on psychotherapy, and in particular CBT, because it has encouraging results and is available, so the message is positive. ✓

This answer also gets the full 3 marks and is clearly focused on the requirements of the question. The answer shows clear understanding of what the leaflet was for and the issues to consider.

■ ■ ■

Issues and debates

Question 6
Definitions

(a) What is meant by 'science'?   (2 marks)

(b) Explain, using one example from your course, what is meant by the 'nature–nurture' debate.   (3 marks)

(a) For this question say what is meant by 'doing science' and what it means to say a study is 'scientific'. In these sorts of questions an example can be useful to show clear understanding.

(b) Explain what is 'nature', then what is 'nurture', and then give an example of some characteristic that can involve both, as this will cover the requirements of the question.

■ ■ ■

Answers

(a) Science is about how something is studied — it must be looked at objectively, in a clearly measured and controlled way ✓ that makes a study replicable so that the findings can be tested for reliability. ✓ There is a theory, a hypothesis comes from the theory, there is testing in a controlled and careful manner, and then conclusions are drawn about the theory. ✓

> This answer gets the 2 marks easily and as shown by the ticks, there is really enough for 3 marks (though the second one on reliability could do with a bit more content).

(b) Nature refers to a person's inherited characteristics from their genes and nurture is about the environment. ✓

> This is clear and gets a mark but there is not enough for more than 1 mark. Nurture needs to be explained more, for example by saying it is about our experiences and learning from the environment. There also needs to be an example, as asked for — such as schizophrenia — pointing out that, while MZ twins share it more than DZ twins, the concordance is far from 100%, so it seems that both nature and nurture play a part.

■ ■ ■

Question 7
Contributions

(a) Compare one contribution from the social approach with one contribution from the biological approach.   (4 marks)

(b) For your course you will have studied two applications from criminological, child, health and sport psychology. Choose one of these and outline a contribution briefly. Then give two evaluation points about the contribution.   (6 marks)

> **(a)** For this answer make four comparison points. The social approach and biological approach are very different in any case (e.g. stressing nurture versus nature) so you could compare in general. Or you could think about how the two contributions you choose help society and then comment on that. There are many different ways you could compare contributions.

(b) There are 6 marks here, so assume 2 for the outline and 2 for each of the evaluation points.

■ ■ ■

Answers

(a) The social approach helps to explain prejudice and the biological approach helps to explain sex differentiation and difficulties with it for the individual. The first is about how people relate to one another and interaction and the second contribution is more about how the individual feels and is about individual differences. ✓ The social approach looks at people in groups to see how an in-group might be hostile towards an out-group, whereas to look at sex differentiation the individual is examined, ✓ with regard to their genes and hormones but also with regard to how they feel about themselves. ✓ The social approach generates theories such as social identity theory by using laboratory experiments (e.g. Tajfel). However, it is hard to check the validity of the findings, as the studies in this case are controlled, whereas the biological approach can look at genes and hormones and studies can be more scientific as well as valid to that extent. ✓ Of course, how the person feels about their gender allocation might not be validly tested by biological means, so the two approaches are very similar when they start looking at experiences ✓ (whether experiencing prejudice or experiencing the 'wrong' gender). ✓

🖉 This answer has been give 5 marks and you would expect to get all 4 comparison marks for an answer with this kind of depth. Some of the marks are for elaboration. The answer has looked at the contributions themselves, and at methods used to study them, which is a good way of making comparison points. A point about nature (biological approach) and nurture (social approach) would be useful as well.

(b) A contribution of the criminological approach is the information found about the unreliability of eyewitness testimony. This is important for society, as it is not helpful to convict someone of a crime they did not commit and also someone else (if the conviction goes wrong) will wrongly go free. ✓ Theories show that eyewitness testimony can be affected by leading questions, by how long there is before recall and by a person's own schemas. ✓ One problem is that the evidence is gathered using laboratory experiments, which means that although there is good reliability, validity is in doubt — as the situations are not real-life ones. ✓ Another problem is that Yuille and Cutshall (1986) showed in a field study that witness recall of a real crime was as good later as it was at the time, so real-life findings contradict the mass of laboratory evidence. ✓

🖉 This answer is good, though the two evaluation points do not seem to be quite enough for 2 marks each. There are clearly 2 marks for the outline so the whole answer gets 4 of the 6 marks. For the extra marks, give an example of a laboratory experiment, such as Loftus and Palmer (1974), and show how it might

not be valid; and add more to the Yuille and Cutshall evidence to show how it was valid.

■ ■ ■

Question 8
Ethics

(a) **A researcher wants to look at how CBT has worked for people with depression. The researcher chooses people who are halfway through their CBT therapy and uses a questionnaire to ask about their experience of the therapy and how it has helped with their depression. Explain two ethical guidelines that the researcher would have to take into account and for each suggest one way that this could be done.** (6 marks)

(b) **Imagine you are talking to a friend about psychology and your friend is critical, saying that animals are used in the study of psychology, which is cruel. Explain one guideline for using animals and how that guideline protects the animals from harm. Then explain one practical reason for using animals in the study of psychology.** (4 marks)

(a) This answer must focus on the scenario given. You need to explain the two guidelines, and this can be without reference to the proposed study; however, it is better to focus on the scenario throughout. Remember to suggest a way of solving the issue — and to do this for both guidelines. There are likely to be 3 marks for each guideline.

(b) This question needs you to focus on the scenario. Just explain one guideline for the use of animals and one practical reason for using animals (2 marks each) — and write as though to a friend.

■ ■ ■

Answers

(a) The researcher has to ensure confidentiality and the questionnaire must not ask for name or other personal information that can identify the respondent. ✓ This is particularly true as these individuals have a mental health disorder and have to be specially protected, as they tend to be a vulnerable group. ✓ It is also particularly true because therapy is in a confidential setting and the relationship and trust between the therapist and the client must not be broken. It is quite simple not to ask for any name or personal information, as in fact the researcher just wants facts and figures about CBT and not about the person as an individual. So the researcher can say this on the questionnaire. ✓

Another issue is about debriefing. This might be hard because a questionnaire tends to be carried out and the data analysed a long time afterwards, so it would not be possible to tell the person what the findings were. ✓ So the findings could be published and then sent to where the data were gathered so that, later, respondents could be informed about the success of their therapy (in general). ✓ Letting someone know afterwards what the study was about is more important perhaps in experiments — the individual in this case can be informed fully before giving consent, so perhaps debrief is less of an issue, and the purpose of the study can be written on the questionnaire. ✓ Having said that, this is a vulnerable group, as already stated, and reading a lot of information on a questionnaire might not be something everyone does, so a debrief is still important. ✓

> What is good about this answer is how it focuses on the research to be carried out and engages with possible issues concerning confidentiality and debriefing. There are more than enough points for the 6 marks. The answer clearly shows understanding of the issues and presents ideas about how to solve them.

(b) I would explain that when anaesthetic is required it must be given and this must be done by someone trained and competent to administer it. ✓ This is to do with the Scientific Procedures Act and forms part of the rules for getting a Home Office licence. If pain is minimised, then using animals might seem less unethical and it surely helps the animals if they are kept comfortable. ✓ You might ask why use animals at all but for practical reasons they are useful. For example, rats and mice (and other animals) have a gestation period that is much shorter than that of humans and so genes can be studied through multiple generations. ✓ It is useful to know about genes — such knowledge helps humans in many ways, such as learning about genetic illnesses like Huntingdon's. ✓

> There are four points here so full marks are likely. The principle of giving anaesthetic is clear and then elaborated to say how the animal is helped — which is part of the question. The practical idea of having multiple generations is explained and then elaborated upon to show why such a feature of animals is useful. This is a well-balanced answer that shows a lot of knowledge and understanding.

■ ■ ■

Question 9
Methods

(a) Compare observations with content analyses as research methods used in psychology. (6 marks)

(b) **Choose two studies you have looked at in detail over your psychology course. For each describe the procedure. Make sure both studies are clearly identified in your answer.** (8 marks)

(a) Here observations and content analyses are chosen because they are the two research methods you may not have covered in as much depth, as your course may not have included either in the content sections. This question is a general one — about the research methods, not actual studies — though you could use studies to make your points. You need to find six comparison points, or elaborate on some so that you can use fewer and still get the 6 marks.

(b) You need to think of two studies and describe their procedures. It is a good plan to start the discussion of each study by stating which study it is. (Although the procedure should make this clear, it is best to make sure.) Assume 4 marks per study and no identification marks.

■ ■ ■

Answers

(a) Observations take place in the natural setting of the participants usually, whereas content analysis is of media content or something similar so not natural in that sense. ✓ Naturalistic observations gather primary data and so do content analyses, though the latter focus on primary analysis of secondary data, which is not the case for observations. ✓ Naturalistic observations often need more than one researcher to test for inter-observer reliability and content analyses tend to need more than one rater as well, ✓ also to test for reliability (to see if they get the same 'scores' from the same material). ✓ (elaboration) Content analyses are limited to existing material, either written or visual or somehow recorded in some form, whereas observations can be done anywhere at any time in any situation, depending on ethical considerations, of course. ✓ Content analyses do not tend to involve ethical issues as the material is already printed and there (though the findings can hurt individuals so that involves ethics). Observations also in some ways do not involve ethics because observing in a public place (where people expect to be watched) is acceptable — but there are still rules about observing ethically. ✓ Observations can involve tallying after categories have been agreed and content analysis can also involve tallying when or if categories become clear. For example, observations can record different behaviours according to gender and content analysis can record different comments according to gender, so they can gather data in a very similar way. ✓

This answer has six comparison points and should show you that this is not too hard. Ethics are a useful way of comparing methods, and other issues chosen include validity (natural setting or not), primary or secondary data, limitations of the research method and reliability. There is 1 mark for elaboration to show that there can be more than 1 mark per point (though in this answer that additional mark is not needed as the 6 marks are gained by the six comparison points).

(b) I have looked at Milgram (1963) who asked for volunteers and brought them to Yale University to take part in an obedience study. However, he said it was about memory. ✓ Then he introduced the volunteers to someone they thought was also a participant, but who was not — this was Mr Wallace. He was supposed to be the learner. The real participant was in the position of teacher and had to ask the learner (a stooge) questions. ✓ It was planned that some answers would be wrong. The real participant had to give an electric shock (a pretended one, but he did not know that) to the learner, going up 15 volts each time ✓ until a machine in front of the real participant started to say 'Danger' and so on. At 300 volts, the learner would go silent (this was planned) and at 450 volts, the machine stopped. ✓

I also looked at Rosenhan (1973) who did a study called 'On being sane in insane places'. He asked eight people (though he was one of them) to each go to a hospital and say they heard a voice or noise in their head. ✓ Other than that, they were to talk about themselves normally. If admitted they were to make observations and take notes to log what happened to them ✓ and what it felt like to be in an institution. For example, they noted what was said to them and when staff attended to patients or how long staff stayed away from patients. ✓

This is likely to get 7 of the 8 marks though there is room for more, depending on what detail is chosen as a mark. There is nearly enough, for example, when saying that eight people went to a hospital, so adding that there were 12 hospitals involved might be enough to get that additional mark; or something could be added about the second part of the study when staff 'spotted' pseudo-patients who were in fact 'real'.

■ ■ ■

Question 10
Key issues

(a) **Why is it important to look at how psychology helps to explain issues that are of importance to society (key issues)?** (2 marks)

(b) **You will have studied one key issue for each of the AS approaches you covered (social, cognitive, psychodynamic, biological and learning) and one for each application you covered (criminological, child, health, sport and clinical psychology). Choose one key issue that you studied and explain it using concepts and ideas from psychology.** (6 marks)

(a) You might not be asked a question like this but it is useful to know why you have studied certain areas in the course. If you are asked a question you are not expecting, like this one, in the exam, just use the knowledge and understanding that you have and say what you think about it.

(b) This is a standard kind of question that you should be prepared for. Be ready also for a more specific question — here you are given a choice of one of the eight key issues you have covered. To get the 6 marks, either give six points or rely on elaboration.

■ ■ ■

Answers

(a) Psychology is the study of mind and behaviour and knowing about ourselves can be of interest in itself. However, psychology tends to focus on problems with mind and behaviour and helping people to understand their problems or to improve their lives. This also covers helping society to improve so that members of the society have fewer problems. So key issues for society are of interest to psychologists — both academic and practising psychologists — so that they can shed light on such issues and perhaps help to do something about them to help both society and the individual. ✓✓

> This answer has enough for the 2 marks, though it is hard to see where they are given apart from giving a double mark at the end. There is a lot of elaboration at the start and the main point of the answer comes at the end, so both the main mark and the elaboration mark are given at the end.

(b) One key issue I have studied is how to treat depression and I have learned that there are quite a few different treatments, including both biological ones and more cognitive ones. Depression could be caused by problems with neurotransmitter functioning. ✓ Drug treatment assumes that this is the case — that if neurotransmitter functioning is put right then depression symptoms will be alleviated. ✓ For example, Prozac entails increasing levels of serotonin, as low levels of serotonin can cause depression. ✓ Such drug treatment can work, though not usually for quite a few weeks, which does suggest that it is not just about altering neurotransmitters. ✓

Another treatment is CBT — often medication and CBT are put together to help someone, at least at the start of treatment. CBT is about considering unhelpful ways of thinking, which are negative automatic thoughts that come from rules and assumptions that are unhelpful for the individual. ✓ These rules and assumptions come from core beliefs that have been learned, often from early experiences. A CBT therapist works with the client, who does homework, and together they uncover negative automatic thoughts and work to rebalance them — which means replacing them (if desired) with more helpful ones. ✓ CBT has been shown to be effective and so has drug treatment.

> There are 6 marks here. Some marks are given quite quickly (such as the first mark) because later there is elaboration that is not then credited. There is a useful evaluation point in the middle (the fourth mark). The comment at the end

about effectiveness is very useful but needs evidence to back it before it gets a mark.

■ ■ ■

Question 11
Debates

(a) **Using two examples in your answer, describe and evaluate what it means to society to say that there needs to be social control.** (18 marks)

(b) **In a recent poll, it was found that women were seen as better when it came to keeping in touch, whereas men were seen as better when it came to lending a helping hand. Discuss this issue using any of the psychology you have studied in your course.** (18 marks)

(a) This question is about social control and you will have studied token economy, classical conditioning and drug treatment as forms of social control, as well as how power is an issue. There are other examples of social control in your course that you could use here instead. As long as you use two examples in your answer, that is fine. However, as well as discussing social control in society, you need to discuss why society needs social control — and you could also consider ways in which social control is not so good, as this would be evaluation. The 18 marks include 12 marks for the content of the essay and 6 marks for how well it is written — whether appropriate terms and good communication skills are used, for example.

(b) This is a very open question and asks you to focus on gender issues and differences between the genders. You need to consider keeping in touch and helping behaviour but you do not have to know specifically about those behaviours — you can bring in general ideas, such as from the approaches, to focus on gender differences. You should use description and evaluation in your answer, so that you are 'discussing' as asked. The 18 marks include 12 marks for the content of the essay and 6 marks for the quality of writing — use of appropriate terms and good communication skills, for example.

■ ■ ■

Answers

(a) Society needs social control so that there is order and so that members of the society work and live together in harmony, without aggression, and safely. Psychology considers forms of social control, both with regard to keeping people safe from others and keeping people safe from themselves. Suicide is an extreme form of harm to oneself, and any such risk, perhaps in someone diagnosed as

depressed, is taken very seriously and steps are taken to prevent such a course of action, even though it might be said that it is someone's right to take their own life. This is an extreme example but illustrates the need for social control — they might have that right but only if their mind is in balance (if they are not of unsound mind).

So society works on keeping people mentally balanced — both for their own sake and for the sake of others. One definition of abnormality in a clinical sense is going against social norms, so it can be seen that social norms are there to control society and this means that people do what others expect, which makes people comfortable.

Drug treatment is a form of social control that keeps people mentally balanced, such as those with unipolar depression, who can be prescribed tricyclic drugs and atypical drugs, which are newer drugs with fewer side-effects. It might be claimed that drugs are a medical 'straitjacket' and are used to control people in a way that seems unethical. However, society (through researchers) continues to look for drugs that have fewer side-effects, which suggests that the social control is for the individual as much as for society. If depression can be alleviated, for example by Prozac, which increases serotonin in the brain and can lift low mood, then people lose fewer work hours and perhaps cost society less in terms of medical fees, all of which benefits society as well.

One problem with drug treatment, though, is that it assumes that low mood comes from problems in neurotransmitter functioning, such as low levels of serotonin, dopamine or noradrenaline, whereas depression tends to be triggered by some important event. This was found by Brown et al. (1986), who used interviews to find out from women what brought about the onset of depression and how social support helped to overcome depression. They found that society can help by providing support.

This is what care in the community programmes do for schizophrenia, where life skills can be taught and support given to help someone with schizophrenia to function in society. Therapy like this is still a form of social control as sometimes someone has to attend such a programme to be allowed to live in the community if suffering from schizophrenia. However, the programme is expensive (it involves a great many support workers) so there is a cost to society as well as a benefit. Drug therapy is one example of social control and care in the community programmes are another — both therapies to help with mental health problems.

Another form of social control is using token economy with prisoners to help to control behaviour. Prisoners are rewarded for behaviour that is desired and they get tokens which they can then spend however they want to — there is some sort of shop system to make sure that they are rewarded with something they desire, which is important. A problem is that such therapy does not translate well into the 'outside' world so behaviour can slip back and, if the behaviour is to do with crime they have committed, there can be recidivism.

So society benefits by controlling those with mental health problems but they benefit too. Society also benefits by controlling those who commit crimes, who could be said to benefit too if their lives improve — but it could also be said that such control was for the benefit of the majority in society.

⬚ This answer is thorough given the time allowed. In a way there are three examples, but the answer explains that one example is about treatments and therapies for mental health disorders and the other example is about therapy for prisoners, so drug therapy and care in the community programmes are counted as one example, with token economy as the other example. One study is mentioned (Brown et al. 1986), whereas more would be useful. There is some evaluation, such as suggesting that drug treatment relies on the 'neurotransmitter' explanation, which might not be right, and also when suggesting that TEP may not be useful in a different situation ('outside'). It is useful to start the essay, as done in this answer, by showing why social control might be seen as needed, as that answers the question. There is also a balance in the argument throughout, trying to show the 'straitjacket' of undesirable control and the 'social support' of desirable control. With regard to the 12 marks for content this is close to being enough, and it is clear that this candidate has covered the course and has a lot of understanding. With regard to the 6 marks for the quality of the writing, there is excellent use of terms and clear use of argument and paragraphing. Overall this answer would be expected to get all or nearly all of the marks.

(b) Gender issues are widely discussed in society. The biological approach suggests many differences between the two genders, including differences in genes, hormones and brain structures. With regard to genes and chromosomes there are fundamental differences — women are XX and men are XY. At about 7 weeks the fetus starts changing from the original XX if a male fetus, and hormonal secretions are different — such as Mullerian inhibiting substance (MIS) being secreted. So the genes trigger the hormones and XX has different triggers from XY. Another difference that is found is in the brain. In general there is a difference in the corpus callosum, for example, and in general women do multi-task more — they use both halves of the brain more and men tend to use one side and then the other. So from the biological point of view, it would not be surprising that women keep in touch and men lend a helping hand more. With regard to those particular examples, keeping in touch is perhaps more about emotions and helping is about physical help perhaps, so that might make sense. On the other hand, people are more than just their biology, as that involves nature but nurture is also important.

The psychodynamic approach offers a suggestion as to why the genders are different. In the phallic stage at about 4 years old, the male child goes through the Oedipus complex (Electra for a girl). This means, briefly, that the boy is jealous of his father because of the father's relationship with the mother, and to overcome his jealousy and his feelings of love for his father (these clash) he identifies with his father, thus in a way becoming his father. This identification is very strong and the boy then does 'male' things. A girl identifies with her mother

in a similar way, to resolve conflict, and she then displays female behaviour. If in a society the females are seen as the ones to keep in touch, then according to the psychodynamic approach, that is what they will do. Males might be seen as stronger and more supporting (less emotional) and so would be looked to to help more. If a father helps and a mother keeps in touch, the male and female children will do the same. However, a lot of the evidence rested on a few case studies, not even of children (except Little Hans), so there is doubt about the reliability and the generalisability of the findings about the Oedipus complex.

The learning approach also discusses gender and suggests that through operant conditioning a child develops by doing again what they are rewarded for. So if a boy is rewarded for not crying and a girl is allowed to cry, without punishment, then males are likely to be less emotional (in this way) than girls. A girl might be rewarded for keeping in touch with friends or might value friends more. A boy might be rewarded for helping out — perhaps if there is something that needs lifting in the classroom, a teacher chooses a boy. Social learning theory suggests that modelling takes place. Social psychology suggests that people prefer those in their in-group and are hostile to those in their out-group. Someone categorises themselves as a member of a group and then compares with members of another group. Self-esteem is raised by being part of a group that society approves of. If women see themselves as part of the 'female' group, then someone might have enhanced self-esteem by behaving in the same way as others in the group — which might be about keeping in touch and caring about friends and family. A male might see themselves as strong and helping. Of course, the poll might have had a biased sample or there might have been demand characteristics that led people to think women should be good at keeping in touch and men should help people a lot.

This is a thorough answer and covers all three AS approaches that looked at gender, as well as adding a bit about social identity theory and a comment at the end about characteristics of surveys. This last comment is a useful evaluation point. Other evaluation points include the one about nature–nurture in the first paragraph and the comment about case study evidence at the end of the second paragraph. There is no more direct evaluation, though the linking in to the source, showing how behaviour such as keeping in touch and helping can be explained by the theory, is application and so more than description. With regard to the 12 marks, this essay shows a great deal of knowledge with understanding, a clear focus on the actual question, and some evaluation, so you would expect close to full marks. There is good breadth and depth — breadth of explanations and depth for most of them (except social learning). With regard to writing quality, there is very good use of terms and the structure is clear, so you would expect all 6 marks there too.